FAILURE

is Just a Setback...

GIVING UP

is Forever

Don't let yesterday's failures stop your tomorrows!

a memoir by

George Castellano

Failure is Just a Setback, Giving Up is Forever
Don't Let Yesterday's Failures Stop Your Tomorrows

Author: George Castellano
Editor: Griffin Mill
Proofreader: Lyda Rose Haerle
Cover Design and Interior Layout: Michael Nicloy

All images contained in this book and on the cover are owned by the author.

ISBN: 978-1-957351-09-4

PUBLISHED BY NICO 11 PUBLISHING & DESIGN,
MUKWONAGO, WISCONSIN
MICHAEL NICLOY, PUBLISHER
www.nico11publishing.com

Quantity and wholesale order requests can be emailed to:
mike@nico11publishing.com
or can be made by phone: 217.779.9677

Be well read.

Printed in The United States of America

To Bobby Geddis, who told me:

"Georgie, you have to see the world."

That is where it started.

You might have heard of the *unrewarded geniuses*, those who were born gifted but never made use of their talents. And then there are the highly educated, those who earned multiple academic degrees but never found fulfillment in their careers. They are the *educated derelicts*.

Then there are those rare individuals who had a dream but were neither gifted nor highly educated. They struggled through many failures and humiliation but persevered until they finally reached their goal. In the end, *Perseverance is Omnipotent!*

While growing up, I had heard stories about individuals who, by determination and perseverance, triumphed over adversity and achieved what seemed impossible. Failure doesn't have to be a destination but rather a temporary stop along the road to success. Dreams can become real. To paraphrase Henry David Thoreau, it's okay to build sandcastles in the air as long as you put foundations under them.

My story starts out in post-World War II America, the 1950s, in an Italian neighborhood in Belleville, New Jersey. We lived in a two-family house with my grandparents and my aunt and uncle. My father was a carpenter who left school in 10th grade. He was intelligent but had a limited education because he never learned phonics. My mother graduated high school and had an average grasp of grammar and spelling. The only time that I remember her helping me with homework was when she told me that "tion" at the end of a word was pronounced, "shun." At home, there was no emphasis on higher education because all of our friends and relatives were blue-collar workers. The only reading materials in the house were a children's encyclopedia and some magazines. There were no bedtime stories, and we were never tucked into bed or kissed good night. Across the street from my house was an undeveloped area of about 25 wooded acres that seemed like a wilderness to a 5-year-old.

Occasionally, a horse was kept tied to a tree there—firing up my imagination, thinking that there were cowboys and Indians in the area. It was 1955, and Walt Disney's *Davy Crockett* was this kid's hero. He lived in the woods, hunted wild animals, and sometimes had to defend himself against Indians. I wanted to have a knife like his and fantasized about defending myself against bears and mountain lions. My imagination was unlimited; I would sometimes wander a half-mile from my house, looking for Davy Crockett's cabin.

Most of my days were spent roaming around the neighborhood unsupervised because my mother was preoccupied with taking care of my baby brother. We lived on the second floor of a two-family house with my grandparents and my aunts and uncles living downstairs. It was an Italian neighborhood where we could easily walk to Greneci's grocery store, Joe the butcher, and Frankie Pantaloon's barber shop. I liked going to the butcher because he would always give me a slice of bologna.

My playground consisted of new houses under construction, where I would climb up ladders to second floors, jump down into basements, and walk on scaffolds. One time I fell off a scaffold two stories high. Luckily, Fat Joe the Barber saw me fall and reached out and broke the fall. Another time, I stole a carpenter's knife and cut a hole in a neighbor's pool. Sometimes I stole tools and took them home for my father, but he made me put them back.

The basement of one of the houses under construction provided me and my friend Judy the privacy to "play doctor." I was five, and Judy, a year older, suggested the game, so I was curious and went along. After we dropped our pants and stared at each other, I was shocked that she had pieces of lint stuck to her private parts. It looked disgusting, and I told her so! Then she tried to brush it off. I was traumatized and felt ashamed that I played doctor with her and couldn't get that picture of lint out of my mind. It wasn't until years later that I would be reminded of that day, as you will see later in the story.

Belleville—"Silva Lake"

Belleville, a.k.a. "Silva Lake," offered numerous opportunities for me to get into trouble.

Everything was within walking distance, providing easy access for this bad boy. The neighborhood fire department was two blocks away and presented an opportunity for another adventure. After a kindergarten trip to the fire department, I remembered how excited I was to see the firemen's outfits, the pole they slid down, and the big fire engine. So, one day I decided to walk to the fire department, and when I went inside, I didn't see any firemen. They were probably up on the second floor, so with no one watching, I stole a fireman's helmet. I proudly walked back to my house, carrying it like a prize, but my parents made me give it back.

Another time my imagination got me in trouble was when I thought that I needed a saddle so I could ride a horse. I knew of a guy, with the nickname, Joe Cowboy, who lived around the block and owned a horse. After seeing all those westerns on TV, I wanted to get a horse; so I went into his garage and stole his saddle.

Over and over, my mother neglected to watch me and would let me roam around alone, oblivious to the potential danger. I was about four years old when I went into one of the houses under construction and saw what looked like rolls of pink cotton candy. It was exciting to jump and roll in it, but not for long because I started to itch all over. I immediately went home, but my parents didn't know what was wrong, so they put me in the bathtub. That's when they saw particles of fiberglass floating in the water and realized that it was insulation that I had played in. For many years I had a phobia of pink insulation, and even when I was a carpenter, I tried to stay away from it.

The worst mishap was when I tried to play Tarzan and tied a rope around a broken cement block and then jumped down into the opening excavated for a basement. As I jumped, I grabbed onto the rope thinking that I could swing like Tarzan, but instead, I fell, pulling the block down on my head.

I didn't get knocked out, but I remember feeling dazed. I slowly got up thinking that my head couldn't bleed because it was made of bone. Then I thought that I better check and reached up to feel if I had a cut, then panicked when I saw my hand covered with blood. I ran home and shocked my mother when she saw all the blood running down my face. She immediately put my head under the faucet in the kitchen sink and saw the large gash. Panicked, she asked what happened, and I told her that a brick fell on my head. Next, I remember going to the hospital with my uncle driving and my mother holding a towel on my head. There, I was stitched up, bandaged, and sent home. Later, when my uncle went to the construction site where I was injured, he couldn't find any bricks. He said that the basement walls were under construction and only "cement blocks" were used.

Toilet training should never happen this way…I was about four years old when I started to poop on the toilet without any adult supervision. One time I used so much toilet paper that I caused the toilet bowl to overflow. I was scared and used the rest of the roll trying to soak up the water on the floor. I remember my parents screaming at me when they saw the floor was flooded and covered with toilet paper. That must have traumatized me, because from that time, until I was ten, I used a lot less toilet paper, and instead used a washcloth to clean myself. The ritual started by first wiping the largest amount of poop into the washcloth, then placing it on the edge of the bathtub, so that my mother could wash it. That way I wouldn't need a lot of toilet paper to finish the job and would never clog the toilet again.

It was unique living in "Silva Lake" (the mispronunciation of Silver Lake). In this working-class neighborhood, poor pronunciation was common. Examples of this were: *engine*, pronounced "injun"; a *donkey* was called a "dunkey"; and *forehead* was pronounced "farhead." The expression *dog-eat-dog world* became "doggie dog world." When speaking to more than one person, "youse guys" meant that two or more people were being addressed. Double negatives were required to express the absence of the positive. For instance, "ain't got nothing" meant that *they didn't have anything*. "Don't have no money" meant that *they were broke. Should have* was butchered to "shoulda." *Would have* became "woulda." Almost any word that ends in "ing" would be pronounced with "in" at the end, for example, "runnin," "talkin," and "studyin." Asking someone, "Did you eat yet?" was butchered to, "Ju jeat jet?" Their reply would often be, "No, ju?" Even money had slang names for different denominations: a ten-dollar bill was called a *sawbuck*, a five-dollar bill was a *fin*.

This was the 50's, and there was a lot of prejudice towards blacks in the Italian neighborhood, and unfortunately, my family was no exception. My father was less prejudiced than most, but in his attempt to justify treating blacks equally, he said that, if you cut them, "they bleed just like us."

Worse yet, my grandfather, a former Dodgers fan, sat me down when I was four and told me not to root for the Dodgers "because they hire ni**ers!" That advice didn't register with me until years later when I learned about Jackie Robinson.

My family's friends, as well as people who provided various services, had nicknames that sometimes identified them by their profession. For instance, the man that delivered Coca Cola was called, "Louie Coca Cola." Our heating oil was delivered by a greasy guy known as "Puggy, the Oil Man." Then there was "Fat Joe the Barber." There were two cowboys, one was just called "Cowboy," the other, "Joe Cowboy." There were more colorful characters, "Joe the Indian," "Cheesecake," "Nicky Nick," "Cheek," "Fats," and "Frankie Pants." Even my uncles were referred to by their nicknames, "Sammy Ike," "Twinkles," and "Ju Boy." Other colorful characters were the gangsters, revered and respected as guardians of our Italian neighborhood. They could help out if an Italian family needed money to pay a medical bill or if cops had to be paid off under the table. When my little sister was hospitalized with pneumonia, they offered my father money knowing that he didn't have any health insurance. They were a significant part of our Italian culture, and my family referred to them with respect.

Like most immigrants, the Italians initially were not easily accepted into middle class America, but as my mother proudly pointed out, "They got ahead more quickly by pointing guns in people's faces."

My gangster Uncle Junior, a.k.a. Ju Boy, was the family hero, making hundreds of thousands of dollars, and generously buying gifts. He bought cars, clothing, and jewelry for friends and family. He was known for giving thousand-dollar tips and living extravagantly. I remember going to his apartment and seeing boxes of money, hundreds of thousands of dollars, in counterfeit bills. He was considered the most successful member of the family, and he was feared and respected in the Italian neighborhood. When the FBI came looking for my uncle, the chief of police in a nearby town would call my grandmother to warn my uncle to get out of town.

There was a lot of criminal activity in Belleville, and my mother knew that I was exposed to a lot of bad influence. She didn't want me to grow up a gangster and knew that Belleville was not a place to raise a kid. She wanted to move away, especially after my grandfather died. So, in the summer of 1956, my mother decided to move to my grandmother's house in Rutherford, New Jersey.

Age 6

My grandmother's house was a single-family house in a nice, middle-class neighborhood. The neighbors were made up of Jews and WASPs, so we Italians stuck out like a sore thumb. In addition to my family, my grandmother, her boyfriend Tony, and my Aunt Jo Ann also lived with us. We certainly didn't fit in and were never allowed to play with the neighbor's kids or never got invited into their houses. Worse yet, when my Uncle Junior, "Ju Boy," was arrested by the sheriff, he listed our address as his residence. So, his name and our address were on the front pages of the Sunday paper—ostracizing us from the neighbors even more.

Because of the circular arrangement in the cul-du-sac where my grandmother's house was located, there was a building lot inaccessible from the street. Luckily, this left us an overgrown half-acre lot to play in. To us kids, it was the wilderness, stirring our imaginations with unlimited possibilities. We called it the "lots." It was where we climbed trees, made forts, and constructed battlefields. There we often played army, which was especially popular in post-World War II America. The local Army and Navy surplus store supplied us with gas masks, utility belts, and collapsible shovels. Besides the battlefields, treehouses, and forts, we dug underground hideaways with secret entrances. From the "lots" we made uninvited excursions into neighbor's yards, sneaking around to avoid the owners. If we were spotted, we would run like hell and never get caught because we knew all the passageways between the yards and over fences.

Rutherford, New Jersey, was a conservative town with no bars and a predominately white, middle-class, Protestant population. I was enrolled in Saint Mary's Catholic School, which consisted of mostly Irish students. It was a big change from the Italian neighborhood that we left in Belleville.

After the summer, I started first grade in my new school, and the first boy that I met, Robert Carscadden, offered me a lady finger cookie. We were only six years old, but it was the beginning of a friendship that lasted a lifetime. Amazingly, fifty years later, Robert, a.k.a. Carr, and I would both be touched by the hand of fate, when I made a random phone call and saved his life.

Age 8 and Third Grade

It was when I was eight years old that a change of events helped shape my future. I became interested in first aid, the way that some kids find sports exciting. I was precocious, reading advanced Red Cross first aid manuals, even though I couldn't pronounce or understand some of the words, like *apoplexy* or *asphyxiation*. More confusing was the mention of a "foreign body in the eye." What the heck was that? A foreigner was a person from another country— how could they be in someone's eye?

That Christmas, I asked for an unusual gift for an eight-year-old boy: a Johnson & Johnson's General First Aid Kit. This was no

kiddie first aid kit. This was the real thing, made to treat industrial accidents. I had seen it on display at a local drug store. When I tried to describe it to my parents, I said that it was made of "IRON" (actually it was light metal) and painted blue and white, with the words "General First Aid Kit" painted in red on the front. I'll never forget that Christmas morning when I got the first aid kit, opened it, and saw the sterile gauze pads, ointments, band aids, and Mercurochrome. Sixty years later, I can still remember the medicinal smell of the sterile contents.

It was also odd—being that I lived in a suburb about seven miles outside of New York City—that I imagined becoming a "doctor" and practicing in a rural area. I pictured myself making house calls on back-country roads while driving a red Jeep.

✶✶✶

Third grade was stressful, mainly because of a teacher who I can only describe as a selfish bitch.

My teacher, Mrs. Sheridan, an arrogant Irish, upset my peaceful world. She would talk about her husband, who had a white-collar office job, and his neatly pressed shirts. She also frequently updated us on her two children's accomplishments. I even remember her daughter's stupid name, Daphne.

Thoughtlessly, she had us make useless presents for our fathers on Christmas and Father's Day. They were gifts designed for white-collared office workers. I remember making a tie clip for my father, a carpenter, who never wore a tie except to funerals and weddings. I felt inferior, thinking that I was the only one whose father didn't work in an office. Another time, that bitch had us make a paper weight for our father's office desks. She really screwed me up, for years to come, when she said that it was disgusting and sinful for boys and girls to sleep in the same room. We only had three bedrooms in my grandmother's house, so with our extended family, my brother and sister had to sleep in the same room with me. Because Mrs. Sheridan could afford a big house, she bragged that her son and daughter always slept in separate rooms. After making me feel that my family was inferior and immoral, I went home and told my mother how disgusting it was that my sister slept in my room and told her to get her out. That started me hating my sister. So to appease me, my mother moved her into my aunt's bedroom. Mrs. Sheridan is probably dead by now, but if she were still alive, I would slap the shit out of her. Feeling inferior wasn't the same as feeling sorry for myself.

Feeling inferior made me mad, and although I didn't really have it that bad, I couldn't stand feeling less than everyone around me. Like the time I needed new shoes for school. In order to save money, my parents drove 20 miles to a discount shoe store in East Orange. The store was owned by an old Jewish man with a heavy accent, selling shoes that were out of style and probably unable to be sold elsewhere. Also, the colors were limited, so the standard black or brown shoes that we wore to school weren't available in my size, and the only color that fit me was burgundy. I had never seen burgundy shoes and hated to be different from my classmates. I begged my parents not to buy them, but they bought them anyway. I had to wear them the rest of the school year. Yes, I know when some of you read this you'll think, why is he complaining when some kids don't even have shoes? Well, the fact I'm writing about this sixty years later shows how embarrassed I was. Feeling inferior or poor is relative to one's perspective and not a reality.

By the time I was ten another sister came along, and now we were really crowded in my grandmother's house. My parents had to find another house but couldn't afford any in the neighborhood. I remember feeling sad, driving around looking at houses, fearful of moving away and never seeing my friends again. Luckily, we found a house in the neighboring town, Lyndhurst, which was only about three blocks away.

Age 11

I was eleven years old when we moved to Lyndhurst in 1961. The house was located on a busy street and had a narrow driveway. The neighbor's house was so close, that opening the driver's side car door would almost hit it, while opening the passenger's side door almost hit our house. The basement was unfinished with thick concrete walls that would make an ideal bomb shelter. Because the Cold War was still present, I started to stock a room in the basement with jugs of water, canned foods, flashlights, batteries, and many other essential items. I always worried about things that most kids didn't think about.

Age 12

The Catholic school experience was beneficial because the nuns kept us in line. There, I learned respect and obedience and the consequences of breaking the rules. Their teachings enforced a strict religious and moral code, resulting in a morbid preoccupation with hell as a consequence of bad behavior. Sex was the most controversial issue, and next to murder, it was the worse sin. I didn't know much about it and was probably behind most of my friends at that time. At around age twelve, my cousin Buppie shocked the hell out of me when he explained how babies were made. He was two years older than me and more knowledgeable about forbidden topics. He was from Jersey City, street smart, and knew a lot about girls. I always thought he was cool, but he went too far when he expected me to believe his explanation on how to make babies. He said that a man sticks his penis into a woman's vagina, and then pees in her! I thought that he was crazy and disgusting, and I didn't believe him. I wouldn't repeat that horrible description to any of my friends, especially knowing how sinful it was for a male and female to expose themselves. Without a doubt, I was certain that my parents would never see each other naked, let alone perform such a disgusting act. I was so horrified that I kept that to myself for about a year. Then one day my friend Mark asked me if I had heard how babies were made. When I said *no*, he told me the same thing that my cousin Buppie said about the man peeing into a woman.

I was shocked and asked, "Where did you hear that?" He said that his older cousin Joey told him that.

I said, "Your cousin Joey is from Jersey City, right?"

He said, "Yes."

I said, "Don't believe him, because my cousin Buppie is from Jersey City, and it's probably a rumor spread around by the kids there."

That was that, and I thought that I put an end to that ugly rumor. However, over the next year I learned the truth and had to somehow sanitize the performance of such an act. I had to accept the fact that my parents did it but hoped that they had never exposed themselves to each other. To maintain an image of my parents' purity, I imagined a scene whereby the act was performed in a hospital. First, a doctor would stand behind the naked man holding a sheet up to the man's neck, covering his naked body. Meanwhile, on the other side of the stretched-out sheet, there was a naked woman, whose nurse stood behind her holding the sheet up against her neck. In that way neither the man nor woman could see each other's naked body. The next step was for the man to walk forward, still covered by the sheet held by the doctor, and penetrate the woman, never once exposing themselves to each other. I thought that had to be the only way, because my parents would never allow themselves to be seen by one another naked. This imaginary sanitized procreation procedure reduced the horror and maintained the image of decency. My innocent, self-conceived idea was soon to be exposed, when the following summer I was walking on the boardwalk with my friend

He was 13 years-old, a year older than me, and more knowledgeable about girls. As we were walking, we saw a young guy and girl walk off the boardwalk, onto the beach, and then went under the boardwalk.

Danny immediately said, "She is going to get screwed."

I said, "How can they do it there? They need to be in a hospital!"

He looked at me with disbelief and then said, "What are you talking about?" When I carefully explained the doctor and nurse routine to him, he thought I was joking, and said, "What? Are you stupid?"

That was it! My world of innocence was shattered...and to think that my parents would commit such an act!

Boy Scouts

At age 12, I joined the Boy Scouts, and my membership was one of my most rewarding experiences. Living seven miles outside New York City, Boy Scouts afforded me the opportunity to escape the urban chaos. I dreamt of hiking and camping, exploring the woods, learning about the flora and fauna. I learned the Scout Oath and could recite it by heart. I was enthusiastic and advanced to the rank of First Class in only one year. Backpacking, hiking, and camping were my best memories during that time. Two scouting adventures stand out, one when I had to earn a Camp Cookery merit badge, and the other during summer camp.

On one of the camping trips, I was scheduled to cook a meal on a campfire for my scoutmaster in order to earn the Camp Cookery merit badge. First, I had to make a fire, then position the rocks around it to hold the pots and pans. My scoutmaster was watching me through all these steps. Next I was supposed to place the food in the pans and water in the pot. I was surprised when I went to get the food out of my backpack and there wasn't any. I was embarrassed, but worse I didn't have any food for the scoutmaster. Luckily my scoutmaster knew me well and anticipated my irresponsibility, so he brought extra food. I know that whatever I cooked was barely edible, but I did get the merit badge.

Summer Camp

I was scheduled to go to the Boy Scout summer camp for one week in July. All the scouts in my troop paired off and shared a 2-man tent, but I chose to sleep alone. I couldn't afford a sleeping bag so I borrowed one from a family friend. It turned out better that I slept in a tent by myself, because I peed the bed every night. Besides not having my own sleeping bag, I didn't have a complete Boy Scout uniform. I only wore the shirt and was embarrassed that I had to wear cut-off shorts made from old pants. During that week, on July 2nd, I turned twelve. That morning, during breakfast in the mess hall, the scoutmaster announced it was my birthday. He made me stand up on a bench so that all the troops could see me and sing happy birthday. I was so embarrassed, especially standing there in my ragged cut-off shorts. Later that night, around the campfire, the scoutmaster carved a wooden paddle out of a piece of wood. Next, he carved out the words "Happy Birthday George." Then he told the 10 scouts in my troop to give me 12 whacks on my butt. I had to bend over and act like it was all in fun, but 10 boys each hitting me 12 times hurt so much that I almost cried.

Jersey Shore, Age 12

I spent my summers at the Jersey Shore since I was six and met kids from all over New Jersey. When I was 12, I hung around the boardwalk up until 10 p.m. One night, I was standing outside a bar called The Parrot Club, when a man asked me if I would help him with his car and he would give me five dollars.

I said, "Yes." So, he led me off the boardwalk down several blocks towards the bay. Then we approached a municipal parking lot, and he pointed to a car that he said was his. He tried to open the door, but it was locked. Then he said that was the wrong car and tried another and the door opened. Next, he said for me to get in the driver's seat, and when he went around the car, I thought that he was going to open the hood. Instead, he got in the passenger side and reached over and tried to lock my door. I immediately unlocked it and started to get out, when he said that he wanted to blow me. I was scared and wasn't sure what that meant, but I knew it was something bad. As I jumped out, a man was walking across the street, holding his kid's hand, when he spotted me getting out of his car. The guy that was with me jumped out and crawled between the cars so we couldn't see where he went.

The owner of the car grabbed me as I tried to get away. I said that the man that ran away tricked me into helping him fix his car and then said that he wanted to blow me. When I saw the shocked look on the man's face, I knew that he believed me. He let me go, then a few minutes later I saw police cars going to the area. I never told my parents what happened, but they should never have let a 12-year-old out by himself at 10 p.m.

Jersey Shore, Age 14

At the Jersey Shore, I met tough kids from Newark and Jersey City. They were called greasers or hoods and acted and dressed differently than my Catholic school classmates. I thought that they were cool, dressed in their leather jackets and Italian knit shirts. The Black Leather Jacket was the symbol of a tough guy—and I needed one if I wanted to establish a new identity. Even though it was summer, I decided to buy a black leather jacket and wear it like a coat of armor. I felt proud and thought that I looked cool, not realizing how foolish I looked wearing it in the middle of the summer. I was excited to show my friends from Newark my leather jacket, but they said that it looked old and broken. I said that it was brand new, but what I didn't realize was that it wasn't leather but made of a cheap vinyl material. I was embarrassed and disappointed because I paid $25.00 for it and didn't have any money left.

The older group of tough guys hung around a dance hall called the Casino Ballroom. They looked cool: smoking cigarettes, dressed in Italian knit shirts, sharkskin pants, and their hair slicked back. I learned some of their names, like JB, who had the biggest arms, and Johnny America. Some of the others and I would often be seen hanging around looking cocky. I hung around outside the ballroom with my friends and watched the guys smoking and flirting with the girls. I envied those tough guys and knew that when I got older, it would be me that the people would envy.

Freshman Year

When summer vacation was over, I returned to school and announced to my friends that I had a new identity: a hood. Instead of dressing like my high school classmates, I chose to dress like the hoodlums that I had met at the shore. I wore wine-colored pants, blue lizard-skin shoes, a sharkskin sports jacket, and high-roll shirts. Because the high-roll shirts were 100% cotton, my mother refused to iron them, so I stayed up at night and meticulously ironed every little winkle out of them. Up till then, I had a part in my hair, which didn't fit the image of a tough guy, so I decided to slick it back. I bought a greasy hair wax called "Dixie Peach," used by blacks to straighten their hair back. Every night I rubbed the Dixie Peach into my hair, then took one of my mother's old stockings and pulled it tightly on my head. To further emphasize my transformation as a hood, I started to answer in the street vernacular, "yeah, man," when responding to a question. I even responded to my mother with the "yeah, man."

Behind the tough guy image there was a secret that I had to cover up—I still PEED the bed, and I was 14 years-old. How could I ever be a real man if I peed the bed, and I was petrified that my friends would find out? To compensate, I needed to become strong and develop muscles, because I was skinny and only weighed 128 pounds. I wanted to look intimidating so that I could overcome my insecurity. Because my parents couldn't afford to buy me barbells, I decided to break into a nearby factory at night and steal them. I rode my bike to the factory, about a mile away from my house, went around the back of the building, and forced open a window. I climbed in, and as I looked around, I felt like a kid in a toy store with all those weights, barbells and dumbbells. I noticed some were finished and painted black, others unfinished with slag still attached. The little red collars that held the plates on the barbells looked as pretty as Christmas ornaments. Stealing was sinful and illegal, and because I felt guilty, I stole mostly unfinished plates. I put the weights in a knapsack and the rest in the big basket on the front of my bicycle, the one that I used to deliver groceries. It was impossible to ride my bike with 50 pounds of weights in the basket and 40 pounds in the knapsack on my back. It was so difficult walking home about a half a mile, trying to balance the bike while carrying the heavy knapsack. While struggling on my way home I thought it would have been so much easier to have saved money and have my parents drive me there, pay for them, and drive me home.

Most people consider me a criminal because I robbed those weights, but to me it was the only way to take control of my life. I was only 14, yet this was the beginning of my becoming the "navigator of my own destiny." Weightlifting was the only way that I knew would compensate for my bed-wetting.

Now that I had the weights, I needed a bench and a rack to do bench presses, so I used my father's carpenter's bench to lay on and his sawhorses to rest the weights. I started out placing the barbell across the sawhorses, then lay on the bench. Next, I grabbed the bar and, in one quick motion, lifted the barbell as it rolled close to the edge. It was dangerous because, if I didn't grab it in time, it would have dropped on my neck. I started lifting every night around 10 p.m., down in the basement where my mother was ironing clothes. Still to this day, whenever I smell the steam from an iron, I get a feeling of déjà vu, reminding me of the beginning of what would gradually build my confidence. I started developing muscles and getting stronger, which helped compensate for my bed-wetting. I wanted to develop a reputation as one of the legendary tough guys whose names were familiar to all of my friends, Billy Nee, Chuancy, Tyrone, Muck Muck, Atay, and Frankie D. Up until then I had poor self-esteem, but by becoming strong I eventually would earn respect. I had no interest in sports and barely passed in school.

Age 13, Eighth Grade

I made a fake cast out of papier-mâché by blowing up a cylindrical balloon, covering it with papier-mâché, and letting it dry. The next day I popped the balloon and had a plaster-like cylinder that I could fit my arm in. I cut a hole in it for my thumb, then painted it flat white to appear as if it were plaster. Next, I got a triangular bandage from my first aid kit and made an arm sling. Then I signed a few names on it, slipped my arm in, and my thumb out the hole. It fit perfectly. The next day I wore it to school, supported by the arm sling, and evoked sympathy from all the nuns. When the 8th period began, I asked my homeroom teacher, Sister Nicholas, if I could have the class sign my cast. When she sympathetically said, *yes*, I whipped off the cast and threw it across the room. She looked at me in shock, not realizing it was a fake cast, and then became mean and said that I made a fool out of all my teachers. Next, she said that I had to go to each teacher's room—all nuns, by the way—and show them the foolish cast that I made. As I went from room to room, Sister Nicholas tried to look serious, but all the nuns couldn't keep a straight face and burst out laughing.

As I entered freshman year, I changed both physically and mentally, empowered by the realization that I was the "Navigator of my Destiny." No one was going to boss me around or bully me. I wasn't intimidated by the tough guys' reputations or the warnings that I shouldn't mess with them. Just because they were feared, they never beat me, and I doubted that they could. My friends were afraid, based on the tough guys' reputations, yet they never even had a fight with them. My mantra was, "I can't be beat until I'm down and out."

I felt just as tough as any of them, although I hadn't established a reputation yet. But within the next few years, I would not only join their ranks, but would become somewhat of a legend.

As a freshman I started to demonstrate my overly confident attitude at school. One day, while I was delivering a message to a nun in a classroom full of seniors, a wise guy named Diaz insulted my wine-colored pants. When I handed the note to the nun, Diaz stood up and shouted, "I don't like the color of your pants."

I immediately shouted back, "I don't like your fucking pants either!"

You could have heard a pin drop. Diaz and I stared each other down.

The nun was shocked and said, "Diaz, sit down!"

I left the room feeling cocky, having proved that I wasn't going to be pushed around by anybody, even if he was a senior. Later that day a few seniors warned me that Diaz was going to get me after school. I was a little anxious, expecting we would get into a fight, but Diaz never came looking for me after school—nor for the rest of the year. After that incident my reputation as a tough kid started to get around. The following year I was playing touch football with a few seniors, and I accidentally clipped one, causing him to trip. He was about 6' 6" tall and weighed about 100 pounds more than me.

When he got up, he was really mad and asked, "Who the f**k clipped me?"

I said, "I think I did it."

He said, "Oh, it's okay, George."

Years later, when that guy was coming home from college, he had to take a bus from Newark to Rutherford. Coincidentally, he sat next to my father who was taking the same bus. As they were talking my father asked where he went to high school.

He said, "St. Mary's, in Rutherford."

My father said that his kids also went to St. Mary's. Then he asked my father our names, and when he said George Castellano, the guy said, "You know, he's really tough." That guy went on to become an NFL linebacker.

Age 14

Another major life-changer was the time that I almost got killed in the Newark ghetto. My friend Murphy and I decided to go to downtown Newark at night to buy high-roll shirts. We were only fourteen, yet my parents had no clue where I went late at night. We had to take a bus down to Newark, about 7 miles away. We went to a men's shop where I bought a brightly colored iridescent jacket, and my friend bought a suit for $28.00. As we left the store, a black teenager approached us and asked if we wanted to buy a leather jacket for $15.00. That sounded too good to be true, but I had to check it, especially after my summer fiasco spending $25.00 on a fake leather jacket. We followed him deeper into the ghetto onto Mulberry Street, then further into an abandoned area.

Suddenly 4 other black guys came out of nowhere. I thought, *holy shit, this is it*. One placed a gun to my head and the other a knife to my neck. The guy with the gun threatened to blow my brains out if I made a move. It was overwhelmingly surreal, like a bad dream, imagining the next day's newspaper headlines would read, *TWO TEENS KILLED IN NEWARK.*

I wanted to act tough and tried to say in a deep voice, "What are you doing?" But my voice came out in a high pitch, as if I inhaled gas from a helium balloon. I was holding a box with a newly purchased sports jacket that cost $11.00, when suddenly one of the guys ripped the jacket out of the box. It was an iridescent orange color, and when the guy held it up to show his friends, nobody wanted it so he threw it back at me. The other guy reached into my pockets and only found 30 cents and handed it back to me. All this time I was frozen in fear and never saw what was happening with my friend. They took his $28.00 suit and any money he had left. Then all five of them left in a hurry and disappeared into the ghetto.

That helpless feeling, frozen in fear, standing motionless with a gun to my head, was like being raped emotionally. Worse than trying to rob my money, they robbed my dignity and security, leaving me with a feeling of dread any time I entered an unfamiliar city. I remember being so unnerved and shaken up that I had a difficult time trying to process what had happened. It felt like I was in a war zone, helpless without any defense. My friend Murphy and I knew that we were in a bad area and got out as fast as we could and headed for the bus station. Between the both of us, we only had 30 cents, just enough to pay for one bus fare. We were desperate to get home, so I said to the bus driver that we were just robbed by five ni**ers, and we didn't have any more money. He said that was okay, and to get on, and he took us home—which was about a 45-minute ride. When we arrived home, I didn't want to tell my father what happened because he had warned me many times not to go down to Newark at night because it was dangerous. He found out because he heard my friend Murphy cursing about his suit being stolen. He called the Newark police who said to come down and make a report. When we got down there, my friend and I had to tell what happened. The police said that they would look for the suspects and call us to return to try to identify them. A few days later they called us, and when we arrived, they brought us down to a room where the suspects were kept. The lineup was shocking, like a horror movie, seeing black guys chained together like animals, their glassy eyes, and their wild afro hairdos matted with dried blood. Their faces were bruised with bloodied lips.

They weren't dressed in prison uniforms, because they were rounded up just before we arrived. They were still in their filthy street clothes that were torn and covered with dried blood stains. They didn't resemble the description that we gave the police, and I think that they just rounded up any street bums to place in the lineup.

While we were there, another shocker was seeing a pretty 14-year-old girl, one that could have been my classmate, picked up and arrested for prostitution.

The entire experience of being robbed and almost killed, then witnessing this subterranean world of brutality and violence, was a far cry from my peaceful, white, middle class, suburban life in Rutherford. I became hyper vigilant and street-smart fast, always keeping my guard up for the unexpected. In order to put the odds in my favor, I tried to make a zip gun using a car antenna as a barrel, then mounted it on a gun stock that I carved out of a piece of wood. It was almost complete, but I couldn't perfect the trigger mechanism.

Eventually I would only enter an unfamiliar place carrying a knife, a short machete, or a gun.

From the age of eleven, Lyndhurst was my hometown, a typical North Jersey town congested with traffic, where it was unsafe to ride a bike. My friend Murphy and I took rides from town to town looking for adventure. We usually did crazy things like floating across the Passaic River in a kiddie pool because we didn't have a boat. The Passaic River was so polluted that no fish could survive in it. The plastic kiddie pool was barely deep enough to hold me afloat with its edge sitting just an inch above the water level, allowing me to cross to the other side if I stood perfectly still and didn't shift my weight.

Another time we saw a house with a *No Trespassing* sign that looked really tempting. Wondering what was inside, we went in and explored every room until we found a strong box. Then we took the box and were going to ride our bikes home and open it there. Suddenly a police car pulled up and the 2 cops got out. They told us to open the box, while they waited to see what was inside. We smashed the box repeatedly with rocks until it finally popped open.

There was nothing of value inside, so the cops said nothing and drove away.

★★★

Since I was six years old, my family had a summer house at the Jersey shore. It was where I first earned money, at age nine, collecting empty soda bottles worth two-cents each. I pulled a homemade cart and walked along the boardwalk and beach looking for discarded bottles in garbage cans. Other times I went around the neighborhood looking on back porches for the empty bottles placed outside. A few years later, I found a more lucrative source of income—going under the boardwalk sifting through sand for dropped coins. There I would crawl through tight spaces, over filthy cigarette butts, through spider webs, and sometimes in spots so narrow that I was barely able to squeeze through. It was so exciting every time I found a coin, especially a quarter. Still, to this day, whenever I see a coin on the ground, I still get that feeling of excitement. I was ecstatic when I found a few dollars' worth of coins, a bonanza compared to the usual quarter I was given for spending money. I couldn't wait to crawl out from under the boardwalk so that I could buy anything that I wanted to eat. It was a big deal because, up until that time, I only had enough money to buy a hot dog. I bought an entire sub sandwich for myself. I remembered having a few bites of a sub before and how delicious they were, but my parents couldn't afford to buy me a whole sandwich. I had wanted a sub of my own for a long time, and now I had enough money to buy one for myself.

When I was ready to order the long-awaited Italian sub, I remembered it was Friday. Because I was Catholic, we were forbidden to eat meat on Friday. I still remember that day, when I was torn between eating that sub or committing a sin.

Another boardwalk scheme of mine was rummaging through the garbage dumpster for shredded tickets from the Casino Pier amusement rides. The dumpster was huge, filled with rotten, stinking garbage—but more importantly, thousands of shredded tickets, some completely intact. I knew if I looked long enough, I would find enough to compensate for the disgusting work of sifting through partially eaten food, dirty Kleenex, and an occasional sanitary napkin. Those tickets weren't for me but instead for my cousins and family friends who couldn't afford to pay for the rides. It was about 55 years later, when my cousin, Vinny, reminded me how excited he was whenever he came down the shore, knowing that Georgie could get him free tickets for the rides.

Apparently, the dominant theme for me during my adolescence was proving my manhood—compensating for my poor self-esteem from wetting the bed. And because I had no other talents such as sports or academic achievements, the only way that I could earn respect was by being tough. I scared the shit out of people because I was willing to fight anybody, anytime—never backing down. I knew that I could establish my reputation as a badass and probably wouldn't have to fight that much.

That tough attitude empowered me with the strength and determination to never admit defeat unless I was down and out and couldn't get up again. This philosophy would become a recurring theme, giving me hope whenever I failed and the strength to keep on going. That was all that I had—it was a suit of armor protecting me, trying to establish my place in the world.

Age 15...Forbidden

One of a teenage boy's rites of passage was to claim his conquests with a girl. There were rumors that certain girls "were easy and put out." Knowing that allowed the boys to be bold and more curious. When my friends told me about a girl that showed them her naked breasts, I had to meet her. I eventually met her, and we arranged a time and place to meet at night. It turned out to be near her house on the side of a church. All we did was kiss, and after a few minutes, I slipped my hand down her pants. I was shocked for a few seconds, when I felt what I thought was lint, reminding me of when I was five and played doctor with that girl who had lint on her privates.

That was the first time that I crossed the "forbidden threshold" from innocence to sin. My Catholic school indoctrination was like a shadow following me everywhere. Eventually I developed a guilty conscience for the sinful act and went to confession to tell the priest. I told him that I was sorry and that I would never do it again.

Gradually I started to despise myself and thought that my lustful desires were a horrible insult to the sacrifice that Jesus made, dying on the cross. I was torn between my biological drives and the Church saying it was a mortal sin. I was too naive to understand that lustful desires were inherent in human nature. I felt like a failure in the eyes of God if I thought about sex, knowing that it was a sin. I started hating myself, which caused problems at home. I stopped going to school and started doing construction work with my uncle. I not only hated myself but also school and my family. I started to become a recluse and didn't want to leave the house. I hated myself so much that I destroyed my few cherished possessions, a little toy monkey called "Chippy" that I had since I was six years old, a set of rosary beads from my grandfather who died when I was five, and a bottle of Canoe cologne. Sadly, those were the only things that I had, so they meant a lot to me. For most of the day, I stayed up in my room, which was in the attic, and lay in bed cursing God. My father came up several times to talk to me; then one time he started to cry. I never saw him cry, which momentarily shocked me out of my depression. I thought that maybe I went too far with this self-pity to bring him to this level of despair.

I blamed God for giving me lustful desires and then punishing me for acting upon them. Up until that time I went to church and confession faithfully and prayed often. I did what the Church taught me and tried to be a good Catholic. I couldn't avoid the testosterone-fueled biological drive that caused me to think about sex, and I was so outraged that I screamed out, "God, I can't kill you, so send Jesus back down so that I can kill him again." This was the lowest point in my life…and I didn't know where to turn.

My parents didn't know what was wrong, but my mother was so disgusted with me that she told my father she wanted me out of the house. He said that he would divorce her before he got rid of me. He was the only one who ever showed me love, otherwise I would have been violent and a career criminal. I wanted to see a psychiatrist, but we couldn't afford one. Eventually we found out that my father's insurance covered admission to inpatient psychiatry at St. Barnabas hospital. That was the best thing for me—to get away from my house and everything that reminded me of my depression. It was like a vacation, being in the hospital away from my family and the toxic verbal exchanges with my mother. I can remember the fragrance of the Dial soap and freshly laundered sheets. At home, we only used ivory soap which had no fragrance. It was the first time I was able to take a shower, because at home all we had was a bathtub.

My first encounter with the psychiatrist didn't go well…he told me that I didn't belong there. He said that my father should have knocked the shit out of me instead. I was mad and said, "Watch what you say to me because I'll kill you if I want too."

The next two weeks were great, like a vacation from the reality that overshadowed my depression. I felt good every day and enjoyed being away from my parents. I remember one day when the psychiatrist gave me medication in the vein in my arm. I didn't know what it was at that time and didn't question it. Finally, at the end of two weeks, I was scheduled for discharge the following day and told to call my father to pick me up in the morning. I didn't want to go home and felt that the psychiatrist didn't help me at all. When I called my father, I told him that he had to pick me up the next day but that I still hated everything.

I remember hearing his tearful voice saying, "Okay, Georgie, I'll try to get you into another hospital as soon as possible."

The next day he came to get me, and I didn't say anything during the ride home. He made small talk and mentioned that my grandmother's friend, Jack Brockhouse, had died. I was in a fog, not knowing how I was going to survive in the same environment that led up to my breakdown. We finally arrived home at around 10 a.m., and I hesitantly walked into the house. My mother was standing in the kitchen and asked me how I felt. Wow, it was like magic, the kitchen walls were a brilliant orange unlike anything that I remembered. I thought that they had painted the kitchen since I was gone, but they said it was that way for years. I had been blinded by my depression; it left me with a drab dull vision of the world.

What happened next—I can't explain. Without saying another word, I went up to my room, grabbed my schoolbooks and walked to school which was a mile away. Although I hadn't been to school for almost two months, I just showed up as if nothing happened. It was a Wednesday, and in two days, we were scheduled to take a biology test. Luckily the next day, Thursday, we were off from school because of a religious holiday, and that gave me time to study. I scored an A on that test, and from that day, my life resumed as if nothing had ever happened. No one ever mentioned my breakdown, and even I forgot about it. Surprisingly, missing two months of school never became an issue, and I was never asked by my teachers or my friends to explain what happened. To this day I still don't know how I made a complete turnaround because, when I left the hospital, I still felt the same as before. Sometimes I think that God had some plan for me, somewhere in the future.

It was about a month after I was home, and things were back to normal, that my father told me what the psychiatrist said to him. He told him that I was given sodium pentothal, a.k.a. truth serum!

He said that while I was under the influence of sodium pentothal, I told him about my sinful encounter with a girl which made me feel disgusted with myself. That was because in Catholic school, religion was shoved down our throats, and it seemed that our human nature was corrupt, and everything was sinful.

Unlike my friends who didn't seem to take religion so seriously, I couldn't live with my feelings of guilt. Because the sinful encounter with a girl started my downward spiral into self-loathing, I abstained from any sexual gratification for the next three years. I must have been so traumatized that I never even thought of masturbation between ages fifteen and eighteen. After that struggle between indoctrinated guilt and natural desire, which caused my breakdown, I stopped going to church.

According to the Church, I had committed the worst immoral act next to murder—sins of the flesh. I was weak in spite of my strict obedience to Sunday Mass attendance, routine confessions, and frequent prayers. No matter how hard I tried, I could never be as good as the Church demanded. I felt betrayed and decided that there was no use trying to be a good Catholic, so now there would be no rules, no guilt, and no religion.

During that same time that I had my break from the Church, another problem began to surface. I was fifteen and plagued with a mild case of acne, causing me to be self-conscious. I didn't want to talk to girls because I felt ugly. I wanted to see a dermatologist, but my parents couldn't afford it, so I had to earn $20.00 to pay for the doctor's visit. Because I was only 15 my father had to accompany me to the doctor's office where I was prescribed Aquasol A, 25,000 units a day, and instructed to follow a strict diet. The dermatologist recommended restricting sugar, oil, citrus, fats, spices, iodized salt, and pork. I followed that strict diet for the next three years and ate the same foods every day: Special K cereal with skim milk for breakfast, white bread with beef bologna for lunch, and either beef hot dogs or plain macaroni without sauce for supper. Day in and day out, I stuck to this miserable diet for three years. This strict bland diet and my abstinence from any self-gratification resulted in a miserable frustrating existence.

There was no pleasure in my life which made me crazy and ready to explode at any time. I was on edge and intolerant of anyone insulting me, ready to strike out for even the slightest provocation. I think the constant irritability I was experiencing made me tough. The only thing that kept me going was the confidence that I could survive on my own and that I was in charge of my own destiny.

Uncle Junior

The next major event in my life at age 15 was when my Uncle Junior was released from Leavenworth Penitentiary after doing six-and-a-half years, some in solitary confinement. Prior to Leavenworth, he had spent half of his life in jail, beginning at age sixteen, when he committed his first armed robbery. As strange as it may seem, he was the family hero according to the stories that I heard about his fearless behavior and his  generosity after successful robberies. He was known to have given thousand-dollar tips and was also a legend in the Italian neighborhood. The first month that he was home he took me under his wing, knowing that I had street smarts and a reputation as a tough kid. One of the first things that he told me was that the director of the FBI, J. Edgar Hoover, was a queer. The Mafia knew it but kept it a secret as long as the FBI left the Mafia alone. Hoover even went so far as to say that there was no organized crime, just fragmented groups of gangsters.

That was back in 1965, and Hoover's homosexuality wasn't made public until after he died. After his death, the RICO laws were created, and the FBI started breaking up the Mafia.

My uncle told me exciting stories about his criminal past and the easy scores. He said that he stuck up a bowling alley and netted over $4,000 back in1959. Another time he robbed a high-stakes illegal crap game that had an armed thug guarding the entrance. He said that he came from the back of the building and crawled on the ground. When he came around the corner the lookout guy didn't see him until my uncle pointed his gun at him. The thug knew he would be killed if he didn't open the door for my uncle. When he opened it, my uncle rushed in, gun drawn, demanding that they all drop their pants plus their wallets, and he got away.

Another exciting escapade was the time that he and his accomplice staked out Bamberger's warehouse, watching the security guard's routine as he walked around the building. They calculated the time between the guard checkpoints where he had to punch the clock. Then, they pulled up with a truck and loaded it with refrigerators, washing machines, stoves, and typewriters.

Another time I saw boxes of counterfeit money, probably hundreds of thousands of dollars. The criminal life seemed exciting, even though you might get caught. But so what? It was more exciting than going to school. Besides, I was a poor student and figured if I got caught, I'd go to jail and be around tough guys like myself.

After my Uncle Junior had been home for a few months, he began to realize that I was interested in the gangster lifestyle. In the meantime, my sister's Godfather was killed, and supposedly his body was buried under Route 80. Within the next few years another three acquaintances were killed by the Mob.

One morning while we were sitting in the kitchen drinking coffee, my uncle told me about a guy who he had planned to kill before going to prison. He said that the guy still thought that my uncle wanted to kill him and that he would try and kill my uncle first. My uncle said that he didn't have to kill the guy anymore, but the guy didn't know that and still might try and kill my uncle. If he did, my uncle said that I would have to kill that guy. When he said that, I was holding a cup of coffee, and my hand started shaking so much that I almost spilled it. I protested that it was a mortal sin to kill, and I would go to hell when I die.

He replied, "A mortal sin, my ass! Don't you love your parents, your grandparents, the family name? It would be a disgrace if I were killed, and nobody killed the guy! You are the only one that I could trust to do it, and you have to promise me that you'll do it."

As I said before, the Church failed me, and sins didn't matter anymore. But murder was more than a little sin. I agreed, and said that I would do it, but didn't realize until later that was the day that I sold my soul to the devil. For the next year, I hung around with my uncle learning the ins and outs of the criminal world. One of my first assignments was to find a nerdy student in my school who knew about electronics. My uncle said that the FBI was starting to use bugging devices to catch the Mafia. If we could develop a device that could cause interference, we could make a lot of money. I knew an older student they called "Peanuts," a short, nerdy, skinny, redheaded kid. I asked him to make a device that could fit in a pack of cigarettes and block any listening devices within a room. It had to be sensitive and leave no doubt as to its performance because if it failed, we might all be killed. We settled on a price of $5.00/each. After a week, he handed me an empty cigarette pack with the anti-bugging device hidden inside. It consisted of a double-A battery, a coil, and a wire. I asked him to show me how it worked. He said to put it in front of a TV and see the interference. I paid him the money, brought it home, and tried it out. It didn't do anything, and my uncle had a fit. He said that if we tried to sell these to the Mob, we would be killed.

My uncle had another scheme that could potentially make a lot of money. He had a plan for me to quit school and get hired as a grocery stock boy in a supermarket. I would use false identification and work there for a few weeks, learning the day the cash was removed from the safe to be deposited in a bank. On that day I would carry a concealed pistol, and my uncle would come in at a given time, and we would take out our guns and rob the money. Then, we would travel from state to state, leaving no trace, repeating the same routine. Innocently, I said that I didn't want to put bullets in the gun, and I just wanted to scare people. He said that I needed bullets to defend myself in case they started shooting at us. I thought that, in a bizarre way, it made sense, but we really couldn't say that we were defending ourselves.

I thought it would be cool to do armed robberies, so I practiced looking in a mirror, pointing my finger as if it were a gun, and making scary facial expressions. That way the victims would be scared shitless and hand over the money. But, before we got started, my uncle changed his mind. He said that he didn't want to break my father's heart, like he did his father's. I realized that he was right because I never wanted to hurt my father and knew someday that I would make him proud.

In the meantime, my uncle gave me a bag to hide for him. It contained about $100,000 in stolen government bonds. Apparently, before he went to prison, he had given the bag to my father to hide. I remember, years ago, my father telling someone that he was paid a visit by a few Mob figures, asking him for the bag of money. He said that he had burned it, just as my uncle instructed him to do. They didn't believe him and threatened him. He said that he would kill them if they didn't leave him alone. Then I realized that the bag of bonds that my uncle gave me to hide was the same bag that my father said that he burned.

I think that the guy that was supposed to kill my uncle after he was released from jail was one of the gangsters that came to my father looking for the bag.

Eventually, I realized how many years my uncle had spent in jail, and he had nothing to show for it. I knew that once you got easy money, it would be almost impossible to go back to work, doing construction work for two dollars an hour. The allure of the easy score, the macho image, showing off with a fancy car, and nice clothes, was gradually fading away. He later got himself into some kind of trouble and was wanted by the FBI. Because he had a dangerous reputation, FBI agents had to pose as telephone repairmen in order to get close enough to arrest him without getting shot. They arrested him, and he went back to prison.

Age 16

I was sixteen when I met my first girlfriend during the summer at the Jersey shore. She was from Jersey City, and in order to see her after the summer, I needed a ride. When we got to the street where she lived, I recognized her friend Lucille. When I asked her if she knew where Betty was, Lucille grabbed my arm and walked me towards Betty's house. Suddenly, out of nowhere, six guys surrounded me; one was Lucille's jealous boyfriend, Tommy D. He confronted me and her, demanding to know why she was holding my arm. She said that she knew me from the summer and that I came looking for Betty. While I was arguing, I tried to keep an eye on all the guys around me. I vaguely remember turning my head suddenly as if someone were trying to distract me. As I continued arguing, the guys suddenly walked away. Lucille said that someone tried to sucker punch me while I was arguing, but apparently it wasn't effective. Then I heard someone up the street saying that he wanted to fight me, while his friend was holding him back. I said to tell him to come over, and I'll fight him, but he didn't break away from his friend's grip and walked away. I found out later that he was the one who sucker punched me, and because it didn't have any effect, he left the group and walked away. His name was Georgie M., and he was nineteen years old. He was awaiting trial for murdering a guy, with a two-by-four, the year before. The rest of the night I hung out with Betty and her friends and earned the respect of all the punks who initially tried to bully me.

I continued to go to Jersey City to see Betty, but always needed a ride because I still didn't have my license yet. I had a friend, Glenn, who always drove me in because he was hoping to meet one of Betty's girlfriends. I started to see Betty twice a month and started to like her a lot. This was my first girlfriend, and the relationship was special to me. Because of my Catholic school upbringing, I was taught that if you liked a girl enough, you should respect her dignity, and sex was out of the question. This twisted sense of morals was the basis of my relationship with women. It was essential to maintain the purity of the girl with whom you had long term plans. This was so ingrained in me that my feelings for her were powerful enough to overcome my biological drives. When we were together all I wanted to do was hug and kiss her. I never got excited, and I saw our relationship as romantic, not sexual, thinking that someday she might be the one I would marry.

My innocence came to an abrupt end one night when I met up with her at a dance and saw a hickey on her neck. I had heard of hickeys but never gave one and wasn't sure if I knew how. She saw me staring at it, partially covered up under makeup. Before I could ask her what was going on, she defensively said that a guy named Sammy gave it to her.

At that point she could have let me down easy, ending it there, and letting me walk away. But no, she had to humiliate me, saying, "Sammy makes me hot when he kisses me, kissing you is like kissing a wall." Then she told me how well Sammy danced and how well Sammy dressed. She said, "You're nothing like him."

That moment in time is carved in stone. I felt castrated by the betrayal and humiliation. I was a fool thinking that I was supposed to maintain her dignity and control my passion because I respected her. Although I still liked her and saw her occasionally, I wasn't sure if she still liked me. Now I was determined to learn how to kiss, so I kissed as many girls as possible during the next year. I still went to Jersey City with my friend Glenn, and sometimes saw Betty with some of her friends. One night we picked up Betty and her girlfriend Diane. I was in the back with Betty, and Diane was in the front with Glenn. After riding around, he parked on the waterfront along a warehouse loading dock. The railroad tracks were recessed in the asphalt, so trains and trucks could both pull up to the warehouse. Because Glenn was preoccupied with Diane, he ignored the parked train way down on the track.

Meanwhile, Betty and I were making out in the back, oblivious to what was going on in the front. Suddenly, Glenn started the car, put it in gear, and yelled out a scream. Next thing I heard was the sound of the car crashing into something, and when I looked up it was the train pushing us down the tracks. Apparently, Glenn didn't see the train start moving because he was preoccupied with Diane.

As soon as I realized what happened, I jumped out the front door pulling Betty and Diane out, while the train was coming to a stop. Luckily the train hit the car in the front on the driver's side, lifting the car and pushing it like a wheelbarrow down the tracks. The damage was moderate on the front fender, and the car was still drivable. The railroad workers ran over to see if we were all right and couldn't believe that we didn't get hurt.

During the times Glenn and I drove around Jersey City, I was sixteen and started smoking because I found out that I could get high from nicotine. I never drank alcohol at that time, so it was the first time that I experienced a buzz. I liked it and soon became addicted. Before long, I was smoking two packs a day, trying to reproduce that initial high. Finally, after 6 months, I quit.

Another time, Glenn and I and another friend were driving around Jersey City when a car in front of us stopped and wouldn't move. I was sitting in the back, drunk as a skunk, when Glenn got out and started fighting with the driver of the stopped car. I watched

Glenn hit the guy with roundhouse kicks that didn't seem to affect him. I got out of the car, went up to the guy, and grabbed him around the neck. As I grabbed him, I lost my balance and inadvertently fell while I was still holding him.

We fell together, and I landed with my head striking the curb. It didn't faze me, so we both got up, and I was able to make friends with the guy and end the fight peacefully. The next day I noticed a little swelling on the side of my head where it hit the curb. I didn't have a headache or any signs of a concussion, but each day the swelling on that side got bigger until my head developed a lopsided appearance. The swelling was doughy enough that I was able to press my fingers into my forehead, making five deep indentations. I thought it was funny and let my friends press quarters into the mushy flesh, leaving an imprint of George Washington.

Another time, Glenn and I went to a bar in upstate New York where the drinking age was 18. I was still 16 and didn't have a driver's license, but I usually carried a fake ID. While we were there, Glenn introduced me to two of his nerdy college friends. We were there for about an hour when, suddenly in a panic, Glen said that his friends were outside being hassled by a bunch of guys. I walked outside alone and saw a car surrounded by 4 or 5 guys. I recognized Glenn's friends in the car and went up to the driver, Mike, and asked what was going on. He looked scared and said that those guys wouldn't let them leave.

I loudly said, "Don't listen to these jerk-offs, and leave if you want."

Suddenly, enraged by my cockiness, the biggest guy in the bunch yelled out, "What the fuck did you say?"

I shouted, "You heard me, you big, fat, ugly motherfucker! Your mother is a fucking whore! I want to fuck your mother and then fuck you up."

I'll never forget the look on his face. The big shot loudmouth was dumbstruck and humiliated and didn't say a word. The other guys didn't say anything either, and all of them walked silently back to the bar with me close to them and staring into their faces.

Jersey City again was the setting for another close call, when two guys wanted me to show them where to buy some pot. While I was hanging on the corner with my high school friends in Rutherford, they drove up, parked, and stepped out, asking if anyone had any pot.

One of the punks had a gun visible in his waistband, which scared the hell out of my friends. I told him that I could show him where to get some pot in Jersey City, but my ulterior motive was to get a chance to see a girl that I liked whose brother was a drug dealer. We got in their car and headed to Jersey City.

Both of them acted like they were high, talking loudly and driving too fast. While driving in Jersey City through a quiet zone near a hospital, two cops jumped out of an unmarked car with guns drawn. The driver stopped, and we were told to get out with our hands up. The punk with the gun threw it back to me, and I quickly threw it under the front seat. As we got out, we were told to put our hands up against the car, and the cop pointed his gun at us. The other cop searched the car and found the gun. Then he opened the trunk and found a couple of chains that could be used as weapons and asked the punks what they were for. They acted stupid and said they didn't know. The cop who found the gun told us to get out of Jersey City and that he was keeping the gun. The two guys decided to forget about the pot and drove me back to my high school friends. It was just another school night that turned out more exciting than just hanging out with my friends.

I started going to karate school at sixteen. This, in addition to weight lifting, added a necessary skill to my street fighting mentality. I paid for my own classes, plus the forty-minute bus trip each way, three nights a week. My parents had no involvement in my extracurricular activities and never asked about my karate classes or my achievements.

Karate was a good outlet for my aggression and helped build my self-esteem. I was a natural at sparring, advancing rapidly and earning the respect of my instructors. I liked sparring with black belts because it was more challenging, and I could see how quickly I progressed. Practicing at home enabled me to advance more quickly and kept me focused on a goal—becoming a black belt. I continued taking classes for about eight months but had to quit because my money ran out. A year later I went to an all-black kung Fu school in Newark, about an hour by bus each way, but eventually quit because I didn't get home until 10 o'clock at night. Kung Fu was great, the moves so fluid and graceful, unlike the rigid katas in karate. Although I never advanced to black belt, my fighting skills were almost on that level. I respected black belts for their performance in demonstrating the katas and their graceful execution of each movement, but I often questioned their ability in a street fight. Most didn't appear to have a killer instinct that would enable them to explosively beat the shit out of their opponent. I knew that I had it and thought that outside the Karate school I could beat black belts. I was a natural fighter, and even without any boxing training, I had a boxing match set up with a golden gloves champ. The match took place in a friend's garage with a number of kids from both the local high schools. The fight lasted about six rounds and ended after I beat my opponent. Unlike my opponent, I was a slugger, not graceful, but vicious, relentlessly punching his head. I beat the golden glove champion and was admired by my friends, but unbeknownst to them, I was so exhausted I couldn't go to school the next day.

The next year I had another test of my fighting skills while working after school at a Christmas tree lot. I went on a coffee break to a nearby diner, and while I was in there, I noticed three guys sitting in the back. They were proudly wearing their high school athletic jackets, the ones with their names printed on them. When I left, those three guys followed me out, and the meanest looking of the group asked why I had been bothering the waitress. I said that I didn't bother the waitress and didn't know what he was talking about.

Showing off in front of his friends, he asked with a demeaning attitude, "Are you looking for trouble?"

When I answered *no*, he said that he was, and started to push me. I pushed him back, defensively, and didn't think that I should hurt him because I wasn't even mad yet. As we kept pushing each other, I knew that I could beat the shit out of him. We started wrestling in the street and then over on the sidewalk. He was on top of me, and I still wasn't mad enough to become vicious until he started punching me on the side of the head. It didn't even hurt me, but when he suddenly grabbed my neck and started choking me, I was ready to take his eyes out, but instead I decided to claw his face. I gripped his face like a bowling ball and clawed downward, inserting my fingers into his nose and lips. He immediately let go and stood up screaming and bleeding, clutching his face. Now it was my turn to teach this bully a lesson and embarrass him in front of his friends and the waitress he was trying to impress. While I was laughing, I did a jump kick to his face, then proceeded to punch his face repeatedly and kick him multiple times in the abdomen and groin. He dropped like a sack of potatoes, with blood oozing from his face, whimpering like a baby. I left him lying on the ground, and calmly went back to work as if nothing happened. The next day in school, a few of my classmates had heard that I was in a fight the night before. The ones that lived in the neighboring town where the fight occurred wanted to know the guy's name. I didn't know who he was, except that his name was

Mike. The next day at school, those same classmates found out his name, and couldn't believe that I beat the shit out of Mike V., the biggest bully and badass in East Rutherford. Shortly after the fight, my name got out, and I developed a reputation as a tough guy in the surrounding towns. I went to the rival high school dances knowing that no one would recognize me. I knew that the senior jocks were territorial and that they would confront any unfamiliar student.

As I approached the entrance they got in my face, and asked me, "Who the f**k are you?"

Calmly, I said, "Georgie Castellano." When I said my name, I'll never forget the look on their faces and their sudden change in attitude. Politely they welcomed me and introduced me to their friends as if I were some kind of hero.

Age 19

Several years later, when I was 19, I returned to my old karate school which was located two towns away. Although I had left two years before, I was surprised to find that during my absence, my tough reputation on the streets grew wider and wider. I didn't know most of the new students, yet they had heard of me. One of the advanced students said that he was from the town next to mine and had heard stories about me. When he found out that I returned to the karate school, he said that he was afraid to spar with me. Even my former Sensei, a 9th degree black belt who had intimidated me two years before, now treated me with respect, and before we spared, he whispered, "Take it easy on an old man."

Two brothers in the karate school were impressed with my natural ability as a fighter and asked me if I would go to New York to meet their uncle, an ex-prizefighter. I agreed. So they took me to a bar in the Bronx where they introduced me to their uncle, a bartender. He was in his mid-sixties, his head bobbed and his nose was displaced from years of boxing. They said that, in his youth, he was an excellent fighter, and he fought Jack Dempsey. Later he trained Rocky Marciano, and now he was looking to train a young fighter again. The two brothers vouched for me stating that I was exceptionally skilled as a fighter. Next, he looked me over and then proceeded to squeeze my arms, press on my shoulders and chest and finally squeeze my legs. I must have met his approval because he said that he could make a middleweight champion out of me if I really wanted it.

When I said that I had to think about it, he snapped back and said, "You don't think about it—tell me, *yes* or *no*."

I said, "No," thinking, *here's a guy who almost made it to the top, and he's now tending bar with his head bobbing up and down.* I knew it wasn't worth the price you have to pay trying to make it to number one.

In the past boxing had been a way out of poverty, attracting young guys who had few alternatives to earn a good living. I had thought about it, and maybe imagined that someday I could become a champ, occasionally sparring with golden glove boxers. It was a validation of one's manhood, but the effort needed to succeed rarely paid off. Around this time, the movie, *Rocky*, was a big hit, as it dramatized the life of a young boxer, portrayed by Sylvester Stallone. When I went to see the movie, I realized that it was a hackneyed plot about a boxing wannabe, and it bored me to death. The unrealistic dream of making it big in boxing had been played out, over and over, in lower income neighborhoods. This universal "rags to riches/a nobody becomes somebody" story, wasn't worth watching. Like many others, I had been there with the same dream of becoming a champion and walked out after only fifteen minutes, knowing exactly how it would end.

All of my street fights were in self-defense and won by my adrenaline-driven desire to attack the person trying to hurt me or an innocent bystander. I embarrassed bullies either by beating them up in front of their friends or watching them cowardly back down when I stood up to them. I was usually passive and tolerated a little harassment until they went too far. That's when I caught everyone by surprise and exploded. Because of my reputation, some of the crazy tough guys wanted to hang around with me. They wanted to impress me by beating up a waiter because they didn't like his mustache, or by harassing a guy because he had a pretty girlfriend. But I was the boss and absolutely forbade anybody from getting hurt for no reason.

Jersey Shore, Age 16 to 19

My reputation at the Jersey shore was established between the ages of 16 to 19, but I didn't know at the time that I was becoming a legend. It was about ten years later when I went down to the Jersey shore to visit my cousin Michael who was working on the boardwalk. During his break we went for a walk on the boardwalk and passed by several of his friends. The next day one of Michael's friends asked him why he was walking with "Crazy George."

Michael asked, "What are you talking about, that was my cousin, Georgie."

He said that he had heard of a guy that they called "Crazy George," but couldn't believe that I was the guy behind the legend. It was years later at a Christmas party that Michael told me about that incident.

Every summer I hung around with kids from North Jersey who were vacationing in Seaside Heights. We would congregate on the beach on Sumner Avenue, and after the summer was over, I went over to visit them at their homes. While I hung around different families on the beach, I met Frankie Vali's ex-wife Patty, and their three daughters. The two youngest girls, Toni and Francine, were twins, about eight or nine years old. Almost every day I would hang out with my friends in that group and occasionally play with some of the kids. After the summer, I visited some of those families, including Frankie Valli's ex-wife and kids, in Nutley, New Jersey. One time when I stopped by to visit Patty and the girls, I rang the doorbell, and to my surprise Frankie Vali answered. I recognized him right away, but of course, he didn't know me. I said that I came to see Patty and the kids. When he asked who I was, I knew that he wouldn't know me, so I said, "I'm Georgie Castellano, Ju Boy's nephew."

Bingo! My uncle's name was the magic word that he recognized because my gangster uncle was known by everyone in Newark and Belleville, including Frankie. Realizing the connection, he said to come on in, and that was that.

Boardwalk

Getting back to the boardwalk, there were several incidents where I expressed my intolerance to bullies. I couldn't stomach seeing people getting hurt and wouldn't think twice about helping them. One night, when I was about sixteen, I was taking a stroll along the boardwalk and saw a crowd in front of a concession stand and was curious to see what was going on. As I got closer, I saw two teenage boys in the concession stand yelling for help, while some big drunk guy was beating them up. Without thinking, I jumped over the counter and choked the shit out of the guy. When the cops came, they saw me holding the guy down and started hitting me with their clubs, thinking that I was the assailant. They then realized that the guy that I was holding was the one that caused the trouble.

Another time on the boardwalk, I noticed a large crowd of people in a panic, backing away. I was wondering what was going on, when I heard yelling and cursing and saw two guys attacking the crowd. They were wild, punching anybody in front of them. I could see the scared look on the people's faces as they backed up. I immediately grabbed one of the attackers and punched the shit out of him until he was out of commission. As I started on the other guy, he ran away before I could beat the hell out of him. I made sure that those punks weren't going to ruin anybody's vacation.

That same summer, I was manager of a poolroom on the boardwalk and had to put up with wise guys on a daily basis. The rule was, *No sitting on the pool tables!* and of course the punks would ignore the rules and do whatever they pleased. Whenever I caught someone sitting on the pool table, I had to emphatically say, "Get off the tables!" If I asked, "Please get off," they would take me for a wimp.

There were a few incidents that I remember when I asked two older guys, one about eighteen and the other about twenty, to get off the tables.

They said, "You *ask* us, don't *tell* us to get off!"

I repeated "Get off! That's the rules!"

They threatened me and said that they would meet me after work. I smiled and said, "I get off work at 5:30, and I leave through that door over there."

They left, and about an hour later, they both came back and said, "Man, you've got heart, we don't want to fight you." Then they both shook my hand.

Another day while working in the pool room, my friend Danny pointed out a supposedly tough guy he knew from Newark named Arty. Arty was wearing a black leather jacket and looked arrogant. As I checked him out, he caught me looking and locked eyes with me. Now neither one of us turned away, when suddenly he broke out in a subtle smile. I couldn't hold back from smiling, too, and walked over to meet him. He introduced himself and said he just came down the shore for a week's vacation.

After talking to him over the next few days, he surprised me and said, "This is why I wear the leather jacket." As he proceeded to take it off, I was shocked to see that his back was severely deformed from what he described as scoliosis. He said, "That's why I wear the jacket, so nobody can see how deformed I am."

The pool room was a constant struggle, confronting wise guys breaking the rules and threatening to throw them out. Usually, they listened knowing that I was serious about not sitting on the tables. One time, when I told a punk named John to get off the pool table, he gave me a hard time. When I told him to leave, he said that he would be back with his friends that night after I got out of work. Later that night, just before closing, my boss noticed a crowd of guys hanging outside.

He said, "Don't go out there, we'll leave through the back door, and I'll drive you home in my car."

I told him, "No way, because nobody makes me go a different way out of fear."

So, as I stepped out to lock the door, I was surprised that all the guys hanging around were my friends, and they had heard that John and his buddies were coming to get me. After a few minutes, I noticed John and his cocky buddies were heading toward me when suddenly a large circle formed around them. John wasn't sure what was happening, then suddenly his eyes widened when he realized he had a welcoming party. He quickly changed his attitude and apologized for the misunderstanding. Watching him cower in front of his friends was so satisfying that I told my friends to hold off. When he tried to shake my hand, I refused, and told him to get the fuck out of here and don't come back. He knew not to push his luck because my guys wanted to eat him alive.

AGE 17

Another boardwalk memory took place on my seventeenth birthday when my ex-girlfriend promised to meet me later that night. I was so excited that day, hoping that she still liked me, and we could get together again. I wanted to make the night one that she would never forget, so I planned on getting tickets to take her on the rides. The only way that I could get those tickets was to scrounge through tons of garbage in the dumpster and look for tickets that weren't shredded. In addition, I asked my mother to loan me a few dollars in case my girlfriend wanted something to eat. I was elated because this would be the first time in months that I had a chance to be with her. Excitedly, I waited at the arranged spot on the boardwalk, watching carefully, when suddenly she appeared with several of her girlfriends and walked by, completely ignoring me! I was so devastated that I didn't have the nerve to ask her where she was going, so I caught up to one of her girlfriends and asked her. She said that they were going to a party at a nearby motel so that my ex-girlfriend Betsy could see a guy that she liked. When she said his name, I exploded because that was the same guy who Betsy said had given her the hickey and made her hot when he kissed her, and that kissing me was like kissing a wall. That feeling of betrayal and humiliation felt as though I was stabbed in the heart. I was furious and had one thing on my mind, vengeance, and I immediately rounded up a gang of ten hoodlums. I found out where the party was and directed the gang to stay in the background and wait until I gave them the signal where to attack. First, I had to see where Betsy was and found her on the first floor, in a room with the door left open, dancing with her friend Sal. Several of her girlfriends were there also. There were a few other rooms with the doors left open, and guys and girls drinking beer. As I walked by, I was invited in and offered a beer, but instead I asked where everybody was from. When they told me the town, I remembered it was the same town that Sal lived in. I asked them how many guys from that town were staying there. They said that their group rented most of the rooms in that motel and that there were at least fifty guys. *Holy shit!* The group at the party outnumbered my guys so I tried to warn them to get back, but instead, they attacked. I got the hell out of there as fast as I could, and observed, from a distance, a crowd of at least thirty guys punching the shit out of each other. Limp bodies were picked up and thrown from the boardwalk onto the beach.

Minutes later, paddy wagons, police cars, and ambulances arrived on the scene. I never found out who was arrested or who went to the hospital, but I knew one thing for sure, my girlfriend's party didn't last very long. For the rest of the summer, I never did see those guys that I recruited to take care of business.

That same summer that I turned seventeen, I was scheduled for my driver's test. Up until that time I drove illegally on a permit without a licensed driver. By the time I was ready to take the test I had a lot of experience driving and was confident that I would pass. When I arrived to take the driving test, the motor vehicle official asked if I was ready. I told him, *yes*, so he got in the car and told me to start driving. I started driving, and without thinking, I put one hand on the wheel and one hand out the window.

The official said, "Son, do you know that you're driving with one hand?"

I answered, "Yes." And I said that I always drove with one hand.

He didn't say anything more until the test was over, and then he said that I failed because of my attitude.

It was no big deal that I failed the test because I continued to drive alone on my permit without a licensed driver. One day I got caught speeding and used another kid's license to keep from getting caught. I knew that eventually one of us had to come clean as to who was driving, so I called my uncle who said that he would take care of it. He made a few calls and then instructed me to tell the kid whose license I used to show up in court and play dumb, saying that he wasn't the driver. At the same time, it was arranged with the state trooper who gave me the ticket to appear in court and tell the judge that he would have to investigate further. Of course, that was the end of that, and I got off as well as the other kid. My uncle had connections with motor vehicle authorities, and anything was possible.

47

An example was the corrupt operation and disregard for safety at one of the motor vehicle inspection stations. When I told my uncle that I needed to get my car inspected, he told me to go to a certain motor vehicle inspection station in North Jersey. There I was instructed to avoid the lines of cars waiting to be inspected and to park on the side of the building. Then I was to ask for one of the inspectors, named Tootsie, and tell him that Twinkles sent me. Next, I was to shake his hand with a five-dollar bill hidden in my palm and tell him that I needed to have my car inspected. The transaction was smooth, and I passed inspection without even going through the line. When I got home and told my uncle that I passed, he jokingly said that Tootsie was so corrupt that you could bring a car in on a tow truck and still have it pass inspection.

Another episode was driving to Atlantic City, when I was seventeen, to see the Supremes. My old girlfriend loved the Supremes. So, we got drunk, left Seaside Heights, and drove my 1959 Chevy convertible to Atlantic City. When we arrived, the cop at the entrance said that the seats were sold out and tried to shut the door. I was furious and said that we drove all the way from Seaside and pushed him out of the way. He backed off and didn't say anything as we walked in without even paying. The place was crowded, and it was hard to see the stage, so I put my girlfriend on my shoulders so that she could have a better look. I can't believe I did that...but at least we got to see the Supremes.

I didn't go out with my ex-girlfriend anymore that summer, but she knew that I still liked her a lot. One night I happened to see her with her friends, and she was friendly and said hello. I think that she didn't want to lead me on anymore and told me that she prayed to God to love me, but she just couldn't. That's when I knew that it was over and that she wasn't just playing hard to get. I felt like a fool thinking that she had really liked me and that she just needed time to realize it. How true were the words in the song, *The First Cut Is the Deepest*. Naively, I thought that when you found the right person, love would go smoothly. Then, I realized how naive I was and felt like a loser when it came to girls. I didn't want to get hurt again, so I avoided any potentially emotional relationships for years and walked away from the girls that I was most attracted to, preferring casual encounters so that I couldn't get hurt.

During the summer of 1967, the entire country went up in riots. My friends and I were fascinated with the military presence in Newark, New Jersey, which was close by, so we decided to go there armed with bats and clubs. I put the top down on the car so that we would be visible, as if we were in a parade. When we arrived downtown Newark, we were shocked—it looked like a battle zone, smoke pouring out of buildings, broken windows, and gates ripped off the fronts of looted stores. There were National Guard vehicles, soldiers, Newark Police, and New Jersey State Troopers. We drove, with my convertible top down, around roadblocks without the police stopping us because we were white, and this was a black insurrection. Apparently, we were not considered the enemy, so we were allowed free passage. The State Police had their back windows removed from their cars so two troopers could point their shotguns out the back windows, while the other Trooper in the front passenger seat had a shotgun pointing out that window.

No one stopped us as we drove through the city; many streets were vacant with burned-out store fronts. We drove aimlessly, gawking at the unbelievable devastation. Accidentally, we turned down a street without any State Police or National Guard present and came upon an unimaginable scene.

There were hundreds of black people sitting on the street and sidewalks, while their burnt down apartment buildings lay in smoking ruins. All the stores were looted so no food was available. There were a few men walking around carrying loaves of bread, handing out slices to the starving people. Here we were, six cocky white guys, driving with the convertible top down, initially setting out to show off how brave we were. We must have looked intimidating by brazenly displaying ourselves in spite of this potentially dangerous situation. As I drove slowly, neither of my friends said a word. I know what I was thinking, and they probably thought the same: *Holy shit—what did we get ourselves into?!*

Thank God the people moved out of the way so that we could pass through. They never said a word to us. Later I realized that those people were the victims of the inner-city rage felt across America. Their anger was fueled by years of squalid living conditions now made worse by the destruction of the little they had.

Looking back, I think it was unfortunate that rioting was the only way for blacks to wake up America—violent confrontation scaring the shit out of white people. It reminded me of the story my mother told me about the Italian immigrants who initially put up with a lot of shit until they stuck guns to people's heads. The blacks had to bring this country to its knees by violence, no longer tolerating the years of injustice. Peaceful marches headed by Martin Luther King Jr. got the blacks nowhere, except a one-way ticket to jail for expressing their freedom of speech. Nonviolence didn't seem to work, and it wasn't until violent uprisings, like the 1967 riots, did any change take place.

Those riots in black communities across the country were the first steps in galvanizing white America to wake up and listen.

I saw the changes in 1970 when I became a union carpenter and the beginning of the government's effort to demand the hiring of minorities in any federally-sponsored project. Failure to comply would result in the forfeiture of any contract. Although many of the minorities hired were poorly educated, they gradually learned the trades, earned a livable wage, and eventually their children became the emerging black middle class.

Runaway Age 17

When I started my senior year of high school, I was bored and wanted to quit. I needed adventure, but my parents wouldn't let me quit. I decided to leave home and drive down to Florida, expecting to get a job, my own apartment, and eventually make a lot of money. In order not to scare my parents, I told my best friend Robert, the boy that I met in first grade (and the one that you will read about later), to call my house at 11:00 at night and tell my parents that I was on my way to Florida. In order to raise money for the trip, I cashed in my coin collection, and when added to my other savings, it came to a grand total of $50.00. That was supposed to cover expenses until I got a job.

I took off late in the afternoon and drove all night and the next day. I made it to Jacksonville, Florida, within 24 hours. I didn't calculate the expenses correctly and started to run out of money as I drove further south. I figured on picking up a hitchhiker and having him help pay for gas. Eventually, I saw a guy with a suitcase hitchhiking and picked him up. He got in and said that his name was Chuck and that he was just released from jail. I told him that I had run away from home and needed to make money fast. He said that he had planned on doing stickups by robbing gas stations and convenience stores and that I could be his accomplice. Next, we bought a gallon of Gallo port wine and drank half-a-gallon each. While we were driving down the beautiful Fort Lauderdale Boulevard, I tossed the bottle out the window. Next thing I knew, I had three cop cars chasing me, so I pulled over. Immediately Chuck got out and started talking to the cops, while another cop came over to my side and said, "We know that you're drunk!"

I gave him my license and registration, and after a few minutes, Chuck got back in the car. The cop gave me my license and registration back and said that we were free to go. I didn't know what Chuck said to the cops, and he never explained how he did it. As we drove off, Chuck said that I looked sleepy, and asked if I wanted him to drive. I said okay, and we stopped, and he took over driving.

I don't know how long we drove when suddenly we crashed into a parked car, causing me to be thrown forward, smashing my mouth on the dashboard. I was in a drunken stupor and wasn't sure what happened, when suddenly Chuck screamed, opened the door, and ran down the street, leaving his suitcase in the back seat. I stumbled out, and as I walked around to the driver's side, I saw the damage to the right front fender and a blown-out tire.

Meanwhile the owner of the car came running out shouting, "You hit my car!"

I said, "I didn't do it! Chuck did it!" and I got back in and drove away.

I don't think that I drove too far, and I vaguely remember crashing, with dirt flying up on my windshield. Apparently, I drove my car down into a ravine. The next thing I remembered was the state policemen helping me out of the car and walking me up to the road. I was so unsteady that they made me sit on the back bumper of their car, when suddenly I started vomiting large amounts of bright red liquid that looked like blood. At first the policemen thought that it was blood, but then they realized it was wine. That was the last thing I remembered before waking up the next day in Broward County Prison. I didn't know how I got there until I felt my swollen lip, and then remembered crashing the car. I'll never forget that hangover and couldn't even smell wine without becoming nauseous for the next five years.

As I lay on the top bunk, I saw a guard pass by and asked what the charges were. He said that I was charged with public intoxication, and the fine was $35.00 or 7 days in jail. It was then, while groggy from this hangover, that I realized there was another inmate in the bunk below. He was about thirty years old. He was rolling a cigarette for himself, and then offered me one. Next, the guard brought us breakfast which consisted of a slice of bologna between 2 slices of white bread. A short time later, I was transferred to a larger cell, housing about a dozen or more prisoners. Their ages ranged from 17 to 60. Some were career criminals charged with serious crimes. I felt confined like a caged animal and disgusted by the other inmates' behavior. One young black guy was masturbating in front of everybody, not embarrassed at all. Other inmates told me stories about their crimes, like blowing a guy's head off with a shotgun. The same guy showed me how to strengthen my hand grip by squeezing a rolled-up newspaper. The food was terrible, so I didn't finish my lunch. As soon as the other inmates saw me leave my tray with food left on it, several of them made a mad dash and fought over it. The coffee was lukewarm so, in order to make it hot, the older inmates took a wire from the TV antenna and plugged 2 wires into an electric socket and the other end into the coffee cup. Some of the older career criminals gave me fatherly advice that has stayed with me to this day.

One of them said, "Kid, always take the lunch box trail."

I asked, "What do you mean?"

The other said, "Look at us and where we are. We always tried to avoid work by scheming and stealing but look where it got us. We wasted our lives, half of it spent in prison. The lunch box trail means to go to work for a living and get paid for an honest day's work."

Jail was worse than I had imagined, and I couldn't stand having my freedom taken away. I couldn't make bail because I had only $3.00 left in my belongings. I was allowed one phone call, so I called one of my best friends, Carl Maak, to send me the bail money, and told him that I didn't want my parents to know that I was in jail. Finally, after more than 24 hours, I got a phone call expecting it was my friend Carl telling me that he was going to send me the money. Instead, it was my father, who was furious, telling me that he wasn't sending the bail money so I would have to stay in jail for 7 days. I pleaded with him to send the money, promising that I would straighten out, and even join the Army, if necessary. He finally agreed and said that he would send the money the next day.

I said "NO! Send it as soon as possible!"

A few hours later a guard shouted, "Castellano, all the way."

I didn't know what it meant. The other inmates said that I was getting released. At least I was free, but I still had to report to court in seven days and plead my case before a judge.

So here I was, with $3.00 to my name and released at night to roam the unfamiliar streets of Fort Lauderdale. The first thing that stood out was the royal palm trees, whose trunks were perfectly round, straight up, and as hard as concrete. I thought for sure that they were fake. Not knowing where to go, I kept walking towards a well-lit area that appeared to be a business district. I had no destination nor any place to sleep, so I slept on a bench in the back of a hotel. At first it was warm enough to sleep outside, but by the middle of the night, it became cooler, making me so uncomfortable that I couldn't sleep much. The next morning, I woke up not knowing where I was, but with only $3.00 in my pocket I knew that I needed a job. I checked out different stores and finally found a restaurant that hired me as a busboy. My job was to clean off the tables, and my pay would be only the tips left by the customers. I was starving, since my last meal was in the jail the day before, so I asked the manager if I could have something to eat when things slowed down. She said *no*, but later in the day I was allowed to have stale cake from the day before. I was so hungry that I ate almost the entire cake. By the end of the day, I was given half of the tips, the other half went to the waitress. The amount that I received after six hours came to about $3.80. I decided that I needed a better job and that crime wasn't so attractive, now that I got a taste of jail. I roamed Fort Lauderdale's downtown streets, which were populated by junkies, prostitutes, and occasional closeted gay men. Back in 1967 homosexuality was a crime, and anyone soliciting a partner was fined or jailed.

There were a lot of weird people walking the streets, but there was one guy that always sat on the bench looking stupid, making eye contact, and rolling his tongue. I thought that he would be an easy target to rob his wallet because he looked goofy. To initiate a conversation, I asked him if he had a car. When he said *yes*, I asked him if I could borrow it, just to see what he would say. He mumbled something, so I didn't want to waste my time talking to him and decided not to rob his wallet.

During this time, I found out where my car had been towed, so I hitched a ride to the junkyard. There I found my car with the right front fender bent in. It didn't look too bad, and I thought it would be inexpensive to fix. When I asked the junkyard man how much it would cost to replace the fender, he said that the car was totaled and offered me $65.00 for it. I was shocked that he offered so little and started to argue with him until he said, "Look, kid, this car is a black and white convertible with a red interior, and only a "ni**er" would buy it."

I decided to take the money because I needed it to get a place to stay and something to eat. But before I left, I opened the trunk and took out the few clothes that I had originally packed for the trip. They had been next to a spare battery in the trunk and were damp and musty. I also took Chuck's suitcase—the one he left in the car after the accident.

Since I had been wearing the same clothes for three days, I wanted to change into clean clothes. The clothes that I had in the trunk were too damp to wear, so I went to a laundromat and put them in a dryer. Suddenly, they started to go up in flames, so I pulled them out and stomped on them. I didn't realize that the battery acid fumes soaked into the fabric, making them extremely flammable. I didn't have any other clothes left, so I opened Chuck's suitcase and put on his clothes. They were big on me, but I had no alternative because I had to throw away my burned clothes.

A few days later I was scheduled to appear in court and had to wear Chuck's clothes—baggy pants and an oversized white tee shirt. When I entered the courtroom, I saw how well-dressed everyone was and knew that I looked out of place. When it was my turn to swear under oath, I stood up, feeling self-conscious because I was dressed like a bum. The judge announced the charges and asked me how did I plead, guilty or not? I told the judge that although I was drunk, I thought that I might have been drugged because I never felt that way from drinking before. He asked me how much I drank that night. I said that I only drank a half gallon of Gallo port wine.

He smiled and said that he was certain that the amount of wine was enough to impair my memory and that I was guilty of public intoxication. Since I had already paid the $35.00 fine, he told me that I was free to go. I thanked him and then asked, "Judge, in the future, when I apply for a job, and if one of the questions on the application asks about ever being in jail, can I lie and say *no*?"

The judge and the entire courtroom cracked up, and the judge said, "Yes, you can lie, because in Florida we erase the records of minors under 18."

So, now I was free to roam the streets with the $65.00 that I received for my car, but still needed to find a job. I hung out in a sleazy part of town and found a cheap hotel which I could afford at $3.50 a night.

One day while hanging out, a well-dressed man approached me and offered to buy me dinner. I was suspicious and said, "What are you, queer or something."

He didn't answer, but in a friendly way, he again offered to buy me dinner. We went into the diner and sat at the counter, and although I was hungry, I couldn't eat much, thinking, *what's this guy's intentions.* I only ate half of the meal, and when I got up to leave, the guy asked where I was going. I said, "Shut the fuck up and pay for the food because if you don't, I'll kill you."

While I continued hanging out in the sleazy section of town, I met a girl who worked in one of the stores. She lived close by and was familiar with the people in the area and knew the regulars. She pointed out two guys that were undercover cops that hung out in this neighborhood. One of the guys was the one that I thought of robbing, the one who sat on the bench looking stupid and rolling his tongue. I couldn't believe it, so I approached them while they were talking to a man. Naively, I said that I heard that they were undercover cops. Immediately the man that they were talking to walked away quickly. The two cops were mad and said that I blew their cover and that they should arrest me. They said that they were ready to arrest the man because he was a queer and was walking around with his zipper down. I said that I was sorry and that I could help them arrest junkies, prostitutes, and queers. They said that it was dangerous on these streets and tried to talk me out of it. I said that I wasn't afraid and could handle myself, and then I showed them my karate kicks. They agreed and said that for every arrest that I helped them make, they would pay me $5.00.

After about a week, my father contacted me and threatened that if I didn't come home, he would come down looking for me. I decided to take a plane home, and when I arrived at the Newark airport, my father was there to meet me. I expected the worst, but he was glad to see me. I think that he realized that I could take care of myself and that I had learned a good lesson.

It had been about 8 days since I ran away and last attended school. The day I returned, I was about 15 minutes late, and my homeroom class had already settled down. I quietly walked in as if nothing had happened and handed my homeroom nun a late slip. She looked at me in disbelief, when suddenly the class exploded, running up and hugging me. While I was gone, they hung a map on the wall with pins stuck in it, predicting my whereabouts during the initial days of my adventure.

After the Florida escapade, I reluctantly stayed in school, knowing that my parents wouldn't allow me to quit. I found a part-time job at night, working in a liquor store, stocking shelves and delivering liquor. In the basement of the store, there were old bottles of brandy which I helped myself to on a nightly basis. Working there was fun considering that I was slightly buzzed and getting paid at the same time.

The rest of my senior year was uneventful, especially because, without a car, I couldn't go anywhere and get in trouble. I managed to finish school, and out of a class of 120 students, I graduated… eighth from the bottom of my class. I never intended to go to college, so I signed up for the Air Force in the spring before graduation and planned on starting basic training that August.

In the meantime, I started working down the Jersey shore as a barker on a concession stand on the boardwalk. The game consisted of a wheel with numbers, and an arrow that spun around, finally stopping on the winning space. I would shout out, to vacationers, to come and try to win a prize. My spiel was, "Hey, come on over! Put 'em down, Win 'em out, Pick 'em out, and Take 'em home!" That job taught me a little about the psychology of gambling and people's attraction to try and beat the odds. Sometimes they kept gambling, spending more money than the prize was worth. A fringe benefit working there was a chance to meet girls. I would call them over, enticing them to try to win a stuffed animal. Even if they didn't want to gamble, I had a chance to talk to them while other people were playing the game. Sometimes I was distracted talking to a girl and didn't pay attention to the winning numbers. When the wheel stopped spinning and a player asked, "What do I win?" I believed that they won because I hadn't paid attention as I swept the quarters off the board. Acting cool, as if I were aware of their winning number, I'd say, "You get your choice of the stand."

This happened to me several times over the course of the summer because I couldn't resist talking to a pretty girl. I realized that I probably wasn't the only one mesmerized by a young girl and eventually took advantage of a guy in the same situation. It happened one night when I met up with a girl that I liked and asked her if she wanted to take a walk on the boardwalk. As we were walking, I asked if she wanted me to win her a prize. When she said that she wanted to win a record album, I looked for a concession stand that had record albums, with a young guy working there and flirting with a girl.

"Watch this," I said to the girl that I was with, and I proceeded to play by putting a quarter down on a number. The wheel spun but stopped on a different number than the one that I picked. Of course, I didn't expect to win with the first quarter. The next game I put another quarter down, and as the wheel spun, I watched the guy focused on talking to the girl. When the wheel stopped, the guy, as I predicted, reflexively swept the quarters away, without looking to see which numbers were winners. I knew that he didn't see which numbers were covered, so acting like an excited winner, I pointed out the album that my friend wanted. Without hesitation, he reached up and handed it over to me. I went back about two hours later and repeated the same scam, with the same guy, and won another album.

Air Force Enlistment: 1968

I continued to work on the boardwalk up until a few days before my enlistment day on August11, 1968. I signed up for four years in the Air Force to work as a security policeman, knowing that the job usually required one year in Vietnam. Because it was a dangerous assignment requiring me to guard our planes by patrolling around the perimeter of the base, I wasn't sure if I would ever return. I really didn't care about dying because I felt that my life wasn't worth much, and to die in combat would at least elevate me to a hero's status. Whether I got killed or not, either way, I still had a four-year commitment and didn't think that I would need my civilian clothes anymore, so I gave them away.

I remember the day of enlistment when my parents drove me down to Newark, and nobody said a word. It was the first time that my mother looked as though she was worried about me. After we said goodbye, I was processed through the routine physical, then put on a bus with a hundred other recruits and headed to Newark Airport. There we boarded a plane and flew to Lackland Air Force Base in Texas to start basic training. Upon arriving there we were told to completely empty out our duffel bags, which I thought I did, but somehow a candy bar was stuck at the bottom, and the drill sergeant found it. He looked at me, and with a heavy southern accent said, "Castellano, you're never going to make it!" The drill sergeant's shirt had the word "Ennis" stitched across the breast pocket, which I thought was his rank, confusing it with the Navy's rank of "ensign."

Later when we were instructed to march, he repeatedly shouted out in a heavy southern accent, "layoff—right, layoff—right." Instead of the familiar left-right, left-right cadence, I thought that he was saying to lay off the left foot and then step with the right.

We were housed in a barracks that held 26 airmen, and about half of them had finished a few years of college. I wasn't used to the regimentation and limited living conditions, having to share the bathroom and laundry with 25 other guys. I developed a cocky attitude, fueled by the intense August heat and loss of control of my own destiny. I hated everything and just wanted to go to war so that I could kill, whether it was right or wrong. I was argumentative, sometimes threatening other airmen even while walking around naked trying to stay cool. I yelled at a guy and called him a spic, telling him to go back to his country.

After the first week, the drill sergeant told us that, by the end of the six weeks, one of us had to master the Air Force manual in order for our group to graduate. The manual was a thick book consisting of several hundred pages of policies and regulations. The drill sergeant asked if anyone would like to volunteer to read the entire manual and represent our group. No one raised their hand, so I thought, *what was the big deal?* I knew that I could read well if I put my mind to it, because back in high school, if I bordered on failing by the last quarter, I could ace my exams in order to avoid summer school.

I knew that mastering the manual was a big responsibility, but at least I could distract my mind from the daily grind. Again, the drill sergeant asked if there were any volunteers, and again, no one raised their hand. So, I said that I would do it!

He looked at me with disgust, and said, "You, Castellano? I don't believe it." Having no alternative, he said, "Here, take the manual."

The six weeks of basic training were grueling, waking up at 5:30 every morning, exercising before it got hot, then going to breakfast. Later, it was learning how to shoot, marching with backpacks, then classroom training. One day while standing at attention, the master sergeant caught me talking. I was in formation with about 200 other airmen waiting to get our paychecks.

The master sergeant pointed to me and said, "Get out of formation and stand up here in front of the group." When I got up to the front, he said, "You like to talk, so start talking and don't stop until everyone leaves." It was embarrassing and scary because I didn't know what was going to happen to me.

After everyone left, he said, "Airman, I want you to write 1,000 times, *I must not talk when told not to do so*, and have it on my desk tomorrow morning."

I was shit-scared that I would be put back in basic training and have to repeat another two weeks. I started writing immediately and even skipped dinner, but by 9 p.m., I was only half done when the lights went out. I was desperate and resorted to asking another airman, Donald Krantz, if he would help me. He agreed to do it for 50 cents, but only after I made sure his handwriting was similar to mine. Since the lights were out at 9 p.m., we had to go into the bathroom and each sit in a separate stall. The toilets had seats, but no covers, so sitting for almost two hours was uncomfortable. I remember wiggling around intermittently, trying to get comfortable because there was no support, and all my weight was on my butt. Finally, by 11 p.m., we were finished and went to bed.

The next morning we were awakened by the drill sergeant's greeting: "Get the fuck out of bed!" As I got out of bed, I noticed that my ass was really sore from two hours of sitting, so I yelled out to Krantz, who slept about three bunks away, "Doesn't your ass hurt from last night?" He reflexively answered, "Yeah," then looked at me, and I thought, *Oh, shit, what did we say?* Suddenly, all the guys around us started laughing, but it was useless to even try and explain.

✷✷✷

It was now nearing the end of six weeks of basic training, and I had read the Air Force manual several times, confident that I knew it by heart. It was my responsibility to know the entire book and pass the test because our group's graduation depended on it. Besides mastering all the information in the book, I had to undergo a rigid and much-feared sentry duty interrogation scenario. This test would reflect the culmination of the drill sergeant's training and our performance as a group.

First, I was stationed at the entrance of our barracks with instructions not to allow anyone to enter without proper credentials. Next, a high-ranking officer, a colonel displaying all his medals, appeared. His rank enabled him to intimidate anyone beneath him, so he tried to bully me into allowing him entry. He grabbed the door, trying to pry it open, screaming, and threatening to punish me for disobeying a commanding officer. At this point, many airmen break and give in, allowing an unauthorized individual to gain entry to a secure site. I wasn't unnerved, and continued to insist that he show me the proper credentials before I would let him in. His ranting and raving went on for about five minutes, when finally, he gave in and presented the official documents proving his true identity.

After letting him in, he fired out a barrage of questions covering all aspects of the rules and regulations. After I answered all of his questions correctly, and the colonel congratulated me, my drill sergeant suddenly appeared. He was secretly observing me the entire time and said that my performance representing our barracks was the best that he had ever seen. He apologized for underestimating me and said he was proud of the way I handled the colonel's attempt to breach the security protocol.

After graduating basic, I was sent to security police school on the same base for an additional six weeks. We were trained like civilian policemen as well as given instructions in military tactics. After the third week during the combat training, the two instructors pulled me out of the group and brought me into their office. I didn't know why, but they took a special interest in me, treating me as if I were an equal. They gave me important fatherly advice on how to keep alive in certain combat situations. Why they singled me out from 100 other airmen, I never did find out.

I finally graduated from security police school and was given a one-week furlough to go home. My father picked me up at the airport and asked me how I liked it. I said that it wasn't what I expected, and I wished that I didn't have to go back. My next assignment was at Wright Patterson Air Force Base, near Dayton, Ohio. When I arrived, I was assigned to SAC, the Strategic Air Command, and my job was to guard B52 bombers. Before I was allowed to work, I had to wait for the transfer of my medical records from Lackland Air Force Base in Texas. I didn't know anyone and was bored, so I walked over to the base library to kill some time by reading magazines. Next to the magazines I noticed a book that caught my eye. It was about a famous bank robber, Wille Sutton, who said that he robbed banks because, "that's where the money was."

I found the book so interesting that I read it in two days. Up until then, I only remembered reading a few books, such as *Huckleberry Finn* and *Tom Sawyer*, but now I was motivated to read more.

Next, I read *1984* by George Orwell, another book so interesting that I devoured it in three days. I liked that book so much, I picked up another by the same author, *Animal Farm*, and read it in two days. That started my reading frenzy, like a hyena voraciously devouring its kill, and because my medical records still didn't arrive from Texas, I was able to read every day. Over the next month, I read many books, slowly enriching my mind. I discovered a whole new world out there, as if I climbed a mountain and each book was another step upward, affording me a better view. As I learned more, I realized how naive and ignorant I had been, which was due to a lack of education, not stupidity. Like a caterpillar slowly shedding its cocoon, I was no longer confined by ignorance, but now free to develop my full potential. I started to see life more clearly, think deeper, and question things as never before.

Originally, my enlistment in the Air Force was the knee jerk reaction from a kid graduating high school without any career goals. Never questioning our involvement in Vietnam, I naively joined the military assuming our country needed to stop communism from spreading around the world. I knew that the Viet Cong were alien-looking Asian people, unlike my fellow Americans, and I didn't think it was immoral to kill them. That warped view of an alien culture was soon eliminated when I saw a *Newsweek* article about the war. In the article there was a picture of a dead Viet Cong soldier lying in the dirt, and next to his body was an open wallet with pictures of what appeared to be his wife and kids. That picture forever changed my perception of war and the enemy—who was no different than me. He probably knew little of his country's reason for fighting a war and, like me, just went along with the crowd. Besides my change of heart after seeing the dead soldier's family photos, all my reading enabled me to become more analytical about routine issues I had taken for granted. I realized how little insight I had in deciding the course that I chose. Feeling more empowered, I wouldn't allow myself to be manipulated like a puppet dangling from the strings of complacency. We were supposedly defending the Vietnamese from a communist takeover, yet the airmen that returned from Vietnam said how much they hated them. They were often drunk and rowdy, telling me what a waste of time our involvement in Vietnam was. That the lack of commitment left me with a bad impression. I joined the Air Force to serve my country, for what I thought was a noble cause, but now I had a different view. It was absurd committing fellow Americans to fight and die in a war without justification. I asked myself, *Why should I waste four years in the military without adding any valuable service to my country?* Even though I had made a four-year commitment to serve my country, I decided that I no longer would do it in the military. I wasn't a pacifist, but I was willing to fulfill my four-year obligation in a civilian setting.

When I told my lieutenant about my decision, he said that I could be put in jail for disobeying orders. He said that I should see a psychiatrist and scheduled an appointment. I knew what I was going to say to the psychiatrist, but before I arrived in his office, I put soap in my eyes. That way I would look despondent, with bloodshot eyes while I explained why I didn't want to stay in the military. I said that it was a mortal sin to kill, and Jesus appears to me in my dreams telling me that is wrong. That was all I needed to say to convince him to suggest that I be discharged. My lieutenant didn't buy it, and said that if I kept refusing to participate, I would be put in jail.

That never happened, so over the next several months I continued reading and I started to visit Antioch College in Yellow Springs, Ohio. Antioch College was the third most radical college in the country, while Berkley in California was the first, and Columbia in New York, the second. There, I was introduced to radical ideas that were lighting my brain on fire. There, I started to carry on intelligent discussions with college students about politics and international issues. I was overwhelmed with the amount of information because I still lacked a well-rounded education. Words like *pseudo* and *phallic* had to be explained to me. I didn't even know the difference between *vegetarian* and *veterinarian*, but I knew I was having an epiphany gathering knowledge by leaps and bounds. My thinking became more radical, questioning racial issues and foreign policies. I realized now, I could see some of the current affairs I had taken for granted, and the misconceptions that were ingrained in our culture.

After the visit with the psychiatrist, my Lieutenant had a meeting arranged with an interrogation officer who asked me why I was hanging around Antioch College. Thinking that he was trying to determine if there was some political motivation, I cleverly answered by saying that I wanted to meet girls. Next, he asked why I no longer wanted to serve in the military. I said that I realized it was a mortal sin to kill, and I didn't want to go to hell when I died. He then posed a hypothetical scenario, and asked, "If the enemy had a gun pointed at you, and you had a gun, wouldn't you shoot to defend yourself?"

To his frustration, I answered, "No, I wouldn't kill him because I would eventually go to hell...I would let him kill me, then I would go to heaven right away." He was stumped and had no further questions, and he dismissed me.

A few weeks later, I was called to report to a meeting, but I had no idea what it was about. When I arrived, I was escorted to a room where six high-ranking military officers were seated. Their ranks ranged from second lieutenant to lieutenant colonel. This looked like something important if these high-ranking brass arranged to meet with me. I wasn't impressed and didn't salute. When asked why I didn't salute, I replied that I no longer followed military protocols and considered myself a civilian. Surprisingly, they weren't angry, and even more puzzlingly, they made me an outrageous offer.

The commanding officer said, "Airman Castellano, we are here today to offer you the career field of your choice in the United States Air Force!" Why they made me that offer, I'll never know, because my placement test scores were only average. Had they been high, I would have been given a position that required an above average score. Again, I surprised the "brass" when I refused their generous offer and emphasized that I wasn't interested in any career in the Air Force. I said that I was determined to avoid supporting the military during the Vietnam War, and willing to accept the consequences.

During this intellectual awakening, I decided to write a letter to my parents explaining the change of heart regarding my military commitment. The letter was unlike anything that I had written before, so my parents doubted that I wrote it myself. It was the first time that I was analytical, posing questions as to why they blindly accepted my enlistment in the Air Force. I wrote that they, like most Americans, just existed, clueless in determining the truth regarding our country's actions. The letter was philosophical, probing into why they blindly accepted American policy, both domestic and international. Of course, they didn't think that I was smart enough to reason and write a letter of that caliber, so they gave the letter to one of the nuns that taught me in high school. She read it, and told my parents, "George wouldn't have been able to write on that level." It was true that the old me wouldn't have had the vocabulary or information to write on that level, but now I was empowered with the gift of reading, unlocking my hidden potential.

Around the holidays I was starting to get homesick, thinking that this would be the first time that I wouldn't celebrate Christmas with my family. Although I didn't accrue enough time off to go home, I thought about how miserable spending Christmas alone would be and became sad and depressed. Finally, Christmas Eve morning I decided that I was going home, no matter what the consequences.

When I told my lieutenant that I was leaving, he said, "Good, I'll have a more peaceful Christmas while you're gone." I hurried to pack my duffel bag and dressed in my Air Force uniform, then hitched a ride to the Dayton airport, and got a flight to Newark. My family never expected me to be home for Christmas, so I kept this last-minute decision a surprise. When I arrived in Newark late in the afternoon, I still had to take two buses to get home to my hometown, Lyndhurst. Finally, around six o'clock in the evening, I got off the bus about two blocks from my house. It was Christmas Eve, and a light snow was falling as I walked toward my house. Usually that's where all my cousins, aunts, and uncles celebrated the traditional family Christmas. Before I reached my house, I stopped at a phone booth to call home, planning on tricking my family into thinking that I was still in Ohio, unable to get home. To my surprise no one answered, so I walked over to the house and there were no cars in the driveway. I figured the only other place that they would celebrate Christmas would be my aunt's house, about two miles away. I decided to hitchhike, and since it was Christmas Eve, with a light snow falling, and while wearing my Air Force uniform, it didn't take long for me to get a ride. A young couple picked me up and drove me to my aunt's house. I thanked them and told them I hoped that this Christmas Eve would be a memorable one, knowing that they had helped a serviceman in need.

I was so excited when I entered my aunt's house, hearing familiar loud voices, and smelling the aroma of cooked fish. Suddenly, I made my entrance, surprising everyone, so much so, that my grandmother thought I was a ghost. In turn, I was surprised when my younger sister Judy ran up and hugged me because we had always fought like cats and dogs. It was the best Christmas ever, especially being that it almost never happened.

As the months rolled on, I read more each day. My lieutenant was getting tired of seeing me not working, so he told me to paint a room. I agreed, then purposely spilled paint all over the floor and myself, maintaining a sloppy appearance. Another time when I was doing a sloppy job mopping the floor, a sergeant told me to stop, and grabbed the mop out of my hands. He said, "Castellano, you better learn how to at least mop a floor, because that's all you'll be able to do when you get out."

After several months I realized that I wasn't going to jail, but neither was I going to be discharged or transitioned to a non-military government job. Finally, by March, I was getting tired of waiting and decided to make a bold move. I decided to bypass the mandatory chain of command and go directly to the base commander, a lieutenant colonel. This base was a "SAC" (Strategic Air Command) base with nuclear bomb-loaded B52 bombers that were capable of flying around the world. I had a secret security clearance because of my original training as a security policeman, and once was given a tour of the underground command center. There, I was able to see the world map of our missile silos and B52 bomber routes. Because of my security clearance, I easily entered the SAC compound headquarters, where the commander was housed and went directly to his office building. When I entered the office area unannounced, the commander's secretary was shocked and threatened to call security. Ignoring her I went directly to the commander's office, opened his door, and burst in. I didn't care that I could be arrested or court-martialed, because I had a statement to make and was willing to accept the consequences

Standing proudly in front of his desk, I said, "I'm a revolutionary, and I'm refusing to participate in our government's involvement in the Vietnam War."

He bolted upright out of his chair, red-faced and angry, shocked by my bold behavior. He said, "Airman, sit down. Do you know that you can spend a long time in jail for that statement?"

I answered *yes*, saying that I was willing to go to jail rather than blindly serve my country during the Vietnam War. Then I told him that it was an unnecessary loss of American lives and money, and that I was no longer going to be a puppet. I told him that I proudly enlisted in the Air Force right after graduation, naive and ignorant, but later realized how futile our efforts were to instill democracy in a communist country. I was willing to fulfill the four-year obligation to my country as a civilian, but not in a role that supported the military. After patiently listening to me, he told me how he bombed many cities in Germany during World War II and probably killed a lot of people.

He said, "It was necessary to stop the Germans from winning the war, the war, they said, that would end all wars, the same lie that they told the soldiers in World War I."

He confessed that he was confused about war, and the lies that were told to the people. He seemed remorseful about his role in World War II, trying to justify bombing German cities. Then he said that he didn't know what to believe, and that my generation might have the right idea: "peace, not war." He told me that his son was my age, and that he, too, was against the war and refused to enlist in the military. He said at first he was disappointed with his son's lack of interest in a military career, but more and more he realized the futility of fighting wars.

Finally, he said to me, "Airman Castellano, you are going home with an honorable discharge."

Then he asked for the name of the lieutenant who was in charge of my section of the security police. I told him it was Lieutenant Strayer. He immediately called Lieutenant Strayer and asked him about my situation.

Then after a minute, he abruptly said, "I want him honorably discharged—ASAP," and hung up the phone. Smiling, he told me that he never questioned our government's foreign policy yet was never sure if they were always right. I think that he appreciated my courage to stand up to the system and challenge what most people never questioned.

The next morning there was a knock on my door, and I was told to report to the medical building for my discharge physical. Then the following day I went to the discharge office and received my official papers, which included an honorable discharge, an application for the G.I. Bill, and a plane ticket home. The personnel in the discharge office said that the discharge process usually took five days, and they never saw anyone discharged in one day.

The next day, I went to the airport and flew to Newark, and from there I had to take two buses to get home. When I entered my house, my parents couldn't believe that I was discharged after serving only eight months in the Air Force. I told them that I was honorably discharged and didn't get thrown out.

That was March 28, 1968, and spring was in the air. That same night I went downtown to see my friends and met a kid selling stolen tape recorders for $5.00. I told him he was stupid to sell openly on the streets, and that he should only sell to me. He agreed, and the next week he showed up at a designated time and place, with five tape recorders worth $60.00 each. I paid $25.00 for all five and figured that I could sell them for least $20.00 apiece. A few days later I took the tape recorders to a private bar in Newark where my uncle's hoodlum friends hung out. When I entered the bar, carrying the boxes of recorders, all eyes were on me.

Then one of the guys asked, "Who the fuck are you, kid?"

I proudly answered, "I'm Ju Boy's nephew," the nickname given to my gangster Uncle Junior.

Wow, it was as if a celebrity arrived, and then they all said, "Come on in, kid!"

The guys welcomed me and asked what I was selling. When I showed them the tape recorders, one of the guys bought all five at $20.00 each, for a total of $100, netting me an $80.00 profit.

It was the beginning of April, and I was already home a week after my discharge. I was getting restless to go to the Jersey shore, although the boardwalk wasn't open yet. I drove down there and found a job in construction but couldn't afford a motel, so I slept in my car. I did that for a week until my old boss said that I could stay in his two-bedroom apartment and start working for him.

When the summer season finally started, my friends were surprised to see me back down at the shore. I was supposed to be gone for four years, and now, I was home for good. One friend nicknamed me "Georgie Time Clock," because I punched in and punched out of the Air Force. I worked as a manager in charge of five concession stands on the boardwalk in Seaside Heights, New Jersey. My job consisted of occasional repairs, but mostly collecting the quarters that the players laid down, trying to win a prize. I put them into a canvas bag and brought them to an automatic counting machine. By the end of the summer, I was able to hold a bag of quarters in my hand, and by the weight, tell how much was in there. Believe it or not, I was able to accurately estimate, within a dollar or two, anywhere between fifty and one hundred and fifty dollars.

Also, that summer I had my first experience with hallucinogens and marijuana. I bought mescaline from a guy named Detroit, who had a limp and walked with a cane. Nobody knew where he came

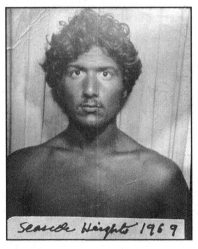

Seaside Heights 1969

from, and after about a month, he disappeared. Another unsavory character asked me to accompany him to buy a kilo of pot in Lakewood where he knew a dealer. We drove there in my car, with a big Gurka knife hidden under my seat. I waited in the car while my friend went into the housing complex to buy the pot, but 20 minutes later he came out empty handed saying that the dealer had no pot left. He said that he told the drug dealer, who was black, that I didn't feel comfortable going into a housing project. The drug dealer said he was going to come out and scare me. I said, "Tell him if he comes out, I'll chop his head off." Then I whipped out my Gurka machete. He changed his mind real fast.

While living with my boss, Ritchie, he informed me that the Chicago mafia wanted to do business with him, involving the concession stands on the boardwalk. His friend, named "Moose," would be the intermediary, arranging the "contracts" for review. As an incentive, the mafia flew in two of their prostitutes from Chicago, one for Ritchie, and one for Moose. Because I had a room in Ritchie's apartment, he woke me one night and told me that he had one of the prostitutes in his room and offered her to me.

While I was working down the shore, my Uncle Junior asked me to see if Moose could contact any mob affiliates to alter the names on stolen government bonds. I gave Moose one of the bonds, but he came back with it and said that none of his connections knew how to do it.

Age 19 Carpentry

After the summer, I joined the carpenters' union where my father was a member. I thought that carpentry would be a good career, and I would follow in my father's footsteps. I had to start as an apprentice, work four years, and then become a journeyman. Ironically, my first job was constructing a building designed to house classrooms on the campus of Rutgers University in Newark. I accepted carpentry as my destiny and liked the challenge of different jobs. My coworkers were like me, rugged and hard-working. One job was unusually dangerous, building concrete support columns under the New Jersey Turnpike. The base column started with a foundation underground, then an enormous adjustable metal form was placed on it and filled with concrete.

After a week, the concrete was dry, and the form was opened by loosening nuts the size of my fists. Next a giant crane lifted the entire form off the concrete column, so that iron workers could attach rebar in preparation for the next concrete pour. As the column grew, the metal form was adjusted so that it would taper inward and straddle the existing column. My job was to ride up, standing on the ball of the crane, holding a three-foot-long wrench, then jump off and hook my safety belt onto the form. With my safety belt secured, I would position myself on the form and would either loosen or tighten the nuts. Eventually these columns would reach up to about 80 feet to provide support for a breakdown lane on the turnpike. I was the only one willing to do that dangerous work.

Another job was working as a carpenter on the new Essex County Courthouse in Newark, where I was given the honorable title of "official coffee boy." In between carpentry, I delivered coffee during the morning and afternoon breaks as well as lunchtime. When I went next door to the old courthouse cafeteria to fill the orders, I saw several secretaries who were also there for their breaks. There was one girl who stood out, so beautiful that it was difficult for me not to stare. I worked on that job for almost six months and saw her five days a week during those breaks. I know that she caught me checking her out during the breaks, but I tried not to stare and make it obvious. I wanted to ask her out but didn't have the nerve. She was perfect, and I was not. Finally, the job was coming to an end, with only one week left, and I would never see that girl again. I struggled with the idea of meeting her but was really nervous about it. Then I thought, *what the heck, it's now or never*. I planned on a day that I didn't get dirty and would approach her at the self-serve beverage counter and ask her out. When the day arrived, I was wearing a clean white tee shirt and felt confident. I watched her as she walked up to get a drink near the same counter where I was filling my orders, and thought, *this is the moment*. Quickly, I turned to her and noticed that she had a slight smile on her face. I was so nervous that all I could say was, "Hi," then choked up, coughed, and a bubble of snot came out my nose. Immediately, I could feel the blood rush to my head, my face turning beet red, exaggerated by the contrast against my white tee shirt.

I said, "Bye," turned around, and quickly walked away. I never returned to that cafeteria and left the job a few days later. It may sound funny, but I can still feel the pain fifty years later.

I started another job with my father, building a new hospital adjacent to the medical school in Newark. I was twenty years old and a second-year apprentice, but I started questioning my future as a carpenter. Although I never planned on going to college, now, after all my reading, I felt as though I was missing something. I'm not sure if my father sensed that I was getting restless, because he asked me to talk to another apprentice, Joey N., who had recently started night school. Even though I wasn't thinking about attending college, after all my reading I was curious about it. I asked Joey if he thought that college was harder than high school. He said it was about the same, but they treat you more maturely. When I asked him if he thought that I was smart enough to go to night school, he hesitated, and then patronizingly said, "Yeah, you could do it." I doubted that I was smart enough to handle college, with my history of barely passing high school. I never thought about another career, and felt comfortable as a carpenter, until one day I saw something that triggered a childhood memory. It was while working on the construction of a hospital that was part of the New Jersey College of Medicine and Dentistry, I noticed a medical student dressed in his white lab coat and stethoscope hanging on his neck. I remembered when I was eight years old and asked for the first aid kit for Christmas. That was so far in the past, and I had forgotten about becoming a doctor, but the idea again sparked my imagination. Just as quickly as it came, the idea of becoming a doctor was soon forgotten.

Around age 19, I experienced a close call—which in retrospect is funny. My younger sister had a friend who always teased me, promising to go out with me when she got older. I really liked her, but didn't want to push her into a relationship if she wasn't ready. One night my sister came home with her friend from a party, and both had been drinking. That was the first time that I saw my sister and her friend drunk. Her friend said, "Georgie, let's go for a ride in your car."

Boy, was I surprised—and eager to go right away. I had a one-track mind and jumped on the opportunity and said, "Let's go!" Off we went looking for a place to park. Finally, we found a secluded spot. What happened next is not what you imagined, because as soon as we parked, and I started to kiss her, she vomited chunks of macaroni all over the car. I headed home as quickly as I could; and for the next two days, I was cleaning pieces of macaroni from under the seats. Was this God's sense of humor, keeping me out of trouble?

Bobby Geddis

The next carpentry job was working at the US Postal Service distribution center in Kearney, New Jersey, where I experienced a turning point in my life. There, I met an older carpenter in his late sixties named Bobby Geddis. Bobby emigrated from Ireland at an early age and was the most knowledgeable person that I had ever met. He was very politically aware as well as opinionated regarding foreign and domestic policies. During the McCarthy era, he was kicked out of the union because he promoted Blue Cross/Blue Shield health insurance. They accused him of being a communist because health care coverage was considered socialized medicine. Bobby filled me in on the hypocrisy in America, opening my eyes to all the lies, and cover-ups.

He started me thinking about the things that I took for granted, making me more analytical in my interpretation of current events. He was the first to tell me about *Aerobics*, a book about cardiovascular conditioning, written by Dr. Kenneth Cooper. That book encouraged me to start jogging before it was mainstream. No one wore Adidas or Nike athletic wear outside of organized sports, so I would jog right after work, wearing my work boots and overalls.

After working with Bobby for about eight months, he said that I needed to get away from my routine lifestyle of hanging out at night and never traveling outside of my area. He was right, because every day after work, I ate supper, washed up, then went out to meet up with my friends. Bobby apparently saw in me something that nobody had ever seen. He said, in his Irish brogue, "Georgie, you have to see the world. Get out of New Jersey and experience what life is like in other places."

That made me think, there *was* a lot more to see, especially now that all the reading had increased my knowledge and broadened my outlook. During this time, I was interested in homesteading, and a man named Scott Nearing and his wife Helen wrote a book on their adventures in Vermont. I had read several of Scott Nearing's books and learned a lot about capitalism, socialism, and self-sufficiency, which they exemplified by their independent lifestyle. Later, I read that Scott Nearing, like Bobby Geddis, was outspoken about American policies, and fired from his job. Scott had taught economics at a prestigious university but was eventually fired because he was against child labor. That was in the early part of the 20th century. Later, he taught socialistic studies at a school in New York City and, coincidentally, I found out that Bobby Geddis had attended his classes.

Gradually, Bobby made me realize how little exposure I had, with a myopic view of life, limited by the comfort of familiarity. Up until now my life consisted of the same daily routine, devoid of any imagination. I could no longer limit myself to the boundaries that surrounded me. Now I wanted to see the world and decided that Europe would be the place to start. I had to save enough money, so in addition to my job as a carpenter, I started selling shirts. I bought them from my neighbor who had truckloads of shirts, four to a box, permanent press, and assorted colors. The shirts cost me five dollars a box, and I sold them for eight dollars, making a three-dollar profit. I sold them at work, standing at the entrance of the building where the workers passed through, and also when I took the orders for the coffee breaks. Within two months I had earned over two thousand dollars, enough to finance a trip through Europe, and told my friend Bobby that I "planned on seeing the world."

1971: My Trip to Europe

I bought a round-trip ticket from New York to London, secure in knowing that at least I had paid for my plane fare back. I was excited, although I didn't know much about Europe, except that it was across the Atlantic Ocean. I figured with $2,000, I would have enough money to buy a motorcycle and travel inexpensively. I also bought a three-month pass allowing me to stay inexpensively at youth hostels throughout Europe. With the pass it only cost about a dollar a night, and sometimes breakfast was included. I budgeted a dollar a day for food, and almost never ate in a restaurant. As foolish as it seems, I had no itinerary, didn't know European geography, and spoke no foreign languages. I was inadequately prepared, yet my parents didn't question my plans, either. I was going alone— carefree and with no time restraints. I remembered the words sung by Janis Joplin, "freedom's just another word for nothing left to lose." I didn't have a girlfriend and had no responsibility to anyone.

Before the trip, my grandmother gave me the address of a friend who lived in England, a woman named Rose, who I had met when I was ten years old. To appease her, I said that I would try to visit her friend, but I really didn't plan on visiting an elderly lady.

I left on May 30th, 1971, carrying only a backpack and two thousand dollars in traveler's checks.

The trip started out by taking a bus to the Port Authority Bus Terminal in New York City. From there, I took another bus to JFK airport, where I boarded my flight to London.

After about an eight-hour flight, I landed at Heathrow airport. Tired from jet lag, I went to sleep early that first night because my biological clock was out of sync. The next day I went to a motorcycle shop and spent a thousand dollars on a new 650cc BSA motorcycle. That left me with only a thousand dollars for the entire trip. I had no itinerary, so I bought a map, and when I opened it, I thought, *holy shit*! I never realized how close the European countries were to each other—France, Germany, Italy, Spain, and Scandinavia. I vaguely remembered reading about them in school, and now I realized some of them were within a day's drive of each other.

I didn't have any schedule yet, so I thought that I would see England first and maybe visit my grandmother's friend. The address was about three hours north of London, in a town called Perry Barr. I wasn't prepared for the changes in weather, thinking that it was spring back home as well as in Europe. As I headed out the first day, I forgot that the British drove on the opposite side of the road and almost got killed. I only had a light-weight red leather jacket offering little protection riding against the cool wind. I was so cold that I decided to cover myself with an orange tarp that I brought along to cover my motorcycle. I attached the bright orange tarp around my neck and chest in order to block the wind. As I drove and picked up speed the tarp billowed out flapping in the wind like Superman's cape. (I can't help but laugh as I write this.) I was cold and still tired from jet lag, so I only drove about an hour from London and decided to rest for the night. I started out the next morning heading for Perry Barr, when suddenly after driving about fifteen minutes, the motorcycle stopped dead. I had no idea what could happen to a new motorcycle, never thinking that I could be out of gas. As I stood on the side of the road another motorcyclist passed by, then suddenly turned around and came back. He was a little older than me and asked what the problem was. I said that I didn't know because it was a brand-new motorcycle.

"You are American," he said, after hearing my accent. Then, he said that his name was Jimmy, and I told him mine. The first thing that he checked was the gas tank, which of course was empty. I couldn't believe it because my motorcycle back home was a Triumph, and it could run for hours on a tank of gas. Apparently the BSA had a smaller tank, which I explained to Jimmy, so he wouldn't think I was an idiot. He said that he would get me some gas and come right back. He returned, and then asked where I was going. I took out the paper and showed him the address in a town called Perry Barr. Excitedly, he said, "I'm from Perry Barr!" He looked closely at the name and address, then turned to me with a look of amazement.

He said, "Rose Hayden and her husband George were my next-door neighbors while I was growing up in Perry Barr."

What a coincidence, one chance in a million. Neither of us could believe it. Then he said, "Follow me, I'll take you there, but first I have to go home and tell my wife."

I followed him home and met his wife and two little kids. I told him that I planned to travel through Europe over the next three months, and I wanted to see England first. After I told him that, he went over to a closet and pulled out a heavy oiled-skin coat.

"Here," he said, "you'll need this while riding your motorcycle in northern Europe." I couldn't believe his generosity.

We took off and headed to Perry Barr, about two hours away. We finally arrived, and although Jimmy hadn't been there since he was a kid, he said it looked the same. We parked our motorcycles and went up to the house. Of course, when Rose came to the door, she didn't recognize either one of us.

Jimmy said, "Rose, it's me, Jimmy—I was your next-door neighbor years ago!"

Her face lit up when she remembered him. Then I told her who I was, and that I had met her when she came to the U.S. to visit my grandmother, Jenny, back in 1960. We explained the amazing coincidence of a chance encounter on the road, and an address we both had in common.

Rose invited me to stay at her house and introduced me to her husband, George. Over the next few days Rose's family showed me around, then invited me to her son's house for Sunday dinner. I'll never forget, while I was at her son's house, there was a movie on TV with Jimmy Stewart and Donna Reed. I didn't know the name of the movie but was captivated by the emotional scenes and superb acting. I never had a chance to finish watching it and didn't know how it ended. Six months later, while I was back home with my family watching TV, I noticed that it was the same movie I saw in England. The movie, *It's a Wonderful Life*, had originally been a flop in 1943, stored away until 1971, and now recirculated as a Christmas story.

✳✳✳

After touring England, I drove to the White Cliffs of Dover, where I boarded a ferry and crossed over to Calais, France. I felt totally free, riding my motorcycle through the French countryside, invigorated by the cool breeze touching my face.

Eventually I arrived in Paris, overwhelmed by the magnificent architecture, but surprised to see the primitive urinals on major streets. The urinals were for men only and consisted of a circular metal enclosure starting about a foot above the sidewalk and extending up to the level of a man's neck. A man would walk into the enclosure, his lower legs and head exposed, and urinate into a funnel, discharging the urine into the street.

I distinctly remember "Boulevard Haussmann," one of the widest and most magnificent streets in Paris. It was one of many streets that radiated out from the Arc de Triomphe, the center of Paris.

About eight years later, when I was in Mexico City, I had a déjà vu experience while walking in the heart of the city. There was a wide street that reminded me of Boulevard Haussmann, the prominent street in Paris. Later when I studied Mexican history, I discovered the street was an exact replica of the Boulevard Haussmann that I saw in Paris. That was because the Austrian Emperor, Maximillian, who ruled Mexico from 1864 to 1867, had the Boulevard built so his wife Carlotta could feel at home.

The second day in Paris, I went to a bakery to buy long loaves of French bread. I parked my motorcycle across the street, hung my helmet on the handlebars, and then went into the bakery. When I came out, I noticed that my helmet was missing, and the only one around was a postman pushing a large cart of mail. I thought that the postman stole my helmet and hid it in his cart under the mail. Because I was on a tight budget and couldn't afford to buy another helmet, I went crazy and attacked the postman. I pushed him aside, jumped in the cart, and dug through the mail, scattering letters in every direction. To my disappointment, my helmet wasn't there, but worse, the postman's sorted mail was in total disarray. Because I didn't speak French, I couldn't explain what I was doing, so I calmly rode off on my motorcycle.

The one regret that I had while in Paris was stopping by the famous Louvre Museum and not going in.

Next, I headed out towards the French Riviera, without wearing a helmet. As I drove, I was bombarded by bugs hitting me in the face. When I finally arrived, I looked like a freak, my face smeared with squashed bugs. I ended up getting another helmet.

After Marseilles, I visited other French cities, and was shocked to see restrooms without a toilet.

The restrooms had just a tile floor, with a hole in it, and old newspapers for toilet paper. On both sides of the hole, there was an outline of two footprints to place your feet while squatting over the hole.

After France, I drove to Spain, stopping in Madrid and Barcelona. I remember distinctly the Moorish influences on their architecture but wasn't educated enough to know the history behind it. While driving somewhere in Spain, I needed to stop and get gas. The cap was positioned on the gas tank just in front of the seat. I sat on the motorcycle while the attendant filled the tank, when he accidentally overflowed it. The gas soaked the crotch of my pants, burning the hell out of my private area. He immediately realized his error, apologizing profusely, while I acted macho trying to hide the pain. Hyperventilating, I fogged up the plastic face shield on my helmet and immediately rode off and looked for the nearest convenience store. I needed to cool off my genitals, but only saw a gas station where I stopped, hoping to buy an ice pop or a cold soda to press against my testicles.

Unfortunately, there wasn't anything cold, so I went into the men's room, pulled down my pants and splashed cold water on my crotch.

✳✳✳

Another time in Spain, I stopped at an outdoor cafe to get a coffee when a young college student pulled me aside so that he could speak in a low voice. He recognized that I was an American and proceeded to tell me how forbidden it was to express any political views in his country. He said Franco, the old fascist dictator, was still in power. That made sense, because I had noticed on, different occasions, the unfriendly way the police acted. They didn't appear as servants of the people but more like an extension of the military. The laws were strictly enforced, and any drug related crime, even marijuana, mandated six years in jail.

After Spain, I was off to Portugal, and spent three days traveling without meeting any English-speaking people. I didn't realize how important it was just to have a basic conversation, even with strangers, and was overwhelmed with a feeling of loneliness. After a few days in Portugal, I returned to Spain along a coastal route and stopped at Costa Brava, a Spanish seacoast. There, I met someone who told me that North Africa was across the water, only a short ferry ride away. I was amazed that the continent of Africa was so close to Europe, separated only by the straits of Gibraltar. Looking out across the water, I saw the massive mountain of rock that I recognized as the symbol for the Prudential Insurance Company. I never knew that the rock was real, I thought it was just a symbol fabricated for an advertisement. Before the trip I didn't even know where North Africa was, let alone have an opportunity to go there.

I took the ferry, crossed through the straits of Gibraltar, passing the Rock of Gibraltar, then reached Morocco, in North Africa. From there, I rode my motorcycle through the rugged Atlas Mountains, encountering Berber tribesmen along the way. Incidentally, Berbers are not Arabs, but descendants of Arian bloodlines, the same as Iranians. Dressed with turbans on their heads and their bodies wrapped in long flowing robes, they walked along the road with their goats by their sides.

They looked like the pictures that I saw in geography books back in grade school, and interesting enough to capture on camera. As I stopped and snapped a picture, they went wild, hurling sharply pointed sticks at me. I gunned the motorcycle and got the hell out of there quickly. Later, I learned that their culture forbade them to be photographed.

As I continued on my way to Fez, the capital of Morocco, it was getting dark, so I set up a tarp and slept in the mountains. Early the next morning, I was awakened by voices speaking a strange language. Luckily, because I was hidden behind some bushes, they didn't see me. Without delay, I took off and headed towards the city of Fez, whose name is noted for the little, round, red hat, with a tassel on top. That hat is easily recognized as the one worn by the organ grinder's monkey.

Along the mountain range there were scarcely any gas stations and very few places to eat. I remember, in the middle of nowhere, stopping at a tent-like kiosk that sold food and drinks. I recognized bottles of coke even though the spelling on the bottle was in Arabic. I bought a coke, a can of sardines and a loaf of bread and made a barely palatable sardine sandwich. Later, farther along the mountain road, I reached an arid area considered high desert. There, I encountered an Arab market bazaar constructed of tents and vendors displaying their wares. The shoppers and merchants were Moroccans, dressed in traditional Arab garb that reminded me of images from the movies.

Amongst the various tents there was one with shoes and sandals lined up outside the entrance. I was curious, and about to step inside, when someone warned me that it was a Muslim Mosque and not to go in with my shoes on. This was so foreign to me; however the educational benefit was an eye-opener, broadening my understanding of a different culture.

Finally, I reached Fez and found a youth hostel. There, I met English speaking Moroccans, dressed in robes, and heads covered with turbans. We sat around a fire pit at night, socializing, while some Moroccans were smoking a communal pipe. In a friendly gesture, one of them handed me the pipe, which I figured contained marijuana. I held it to my lips, and inhaled deeply, then suddenly my knees buckled, and I had to sit down. My head was spinning, and whatever was in that pipe certainly *wasn't* marijuana.

The next day, I went to an open-air market where there were traditional foods cooked on wood fires and cauldrons of curdled milk with flies swarming nearby. Then I saw some Moroccan men dip a ladle in the milk and drink it. As an American, I thought it would be cool to fit in with the Moroccans and drink the communal curdled milk. I dipped the ladle in and took a big swallow of disgusting, soured fermented milk. As horrible as it was, I tried not to show it, straining to keep a straight face.

North Africa was a real cultural shock, and I felt as if I went back in time. I was intrigued, but overwhelmed by their strange culture, so I was glad to return to Spain.

I took the ferry back to Spain, and upon arrival I went through customs, where I retrieved my motorcycle. As I went through the line of vehicles, I was approached by a man clothed in traditional Arab garb with long hair and a beard. I was surprised when he spoke to me in English, because I thought for sure he was an Arab. He realized that I was American and asked me where I was from. When I answered New Jersey, he took out an address book and asked me if I knew of a town called Lyndhurst. Just like my English friend, Jimmy, who was shocked by the familiar address in Perry Barr, I was also shocked because Lyndhurst was my hometown. Even more amazing, he showed me the name of his former college roommate who lived in Lyndhurst. I was shocked, and said that I knew his friend, and that he owned a gym in Lyndhurst. We were both amazed and couldn't believe this chance meeting thousands of miles from home. These two amazing coincidences worlds apart, experienced by one person in a short time, are unbelievable—may be God's sense of humor. Jumping ahead, months later when I returned home from my trip, I stopped by the gym that his friend owned. I told him about my encounter in Europe, with a man dressed like an Arab, who asked me where I was from. When I told him New Jersey, he asked me where in Jersey. I told him, Lyndhurst. He then proceeded to take out an address book with your name and address and asked if I knew this person, "Joey M." I told him that I had heard of you and that you owned a gym. He said that he was a former college roommate, but he didn't tell me his name. To Joey's surprise and mine, he figured out who the guy dressed like an Arab was. He said that he had met him in college and that he was the heir to the Popsicle enterprise.

While heading back through Spain I stopped to get gas, and as I drove away, I collided with a car. Its rear bumper caught the front brake cable on my motorcycle and flipped me and the motorcycle up in the air. I didn't get hurt, but my bike had a broken headlight and some oil leaked out. As soon as I got up and lifted my motorcycle, the driver of the car ran over to me and tried to tell me something in

Spanish. I didn't understand him, when suddenly another man who spoke English translated the driver's Spanish to me. He said the law in Spain mandated that the drivers of both vehicles in a collision be detained by the police until all their paperwork cleared. The man translating said that the driver of the car knew a local mechanic who could fix my light and replace the oil, avoiding any police involvement. I was able to follow him to the mechanic's garage where they fixed the headlight and replaced the oil; then I was back on the road again.

It was about the third day in Spain, after returning from Morocco, that I started to get sick with a fever and stomach cramps. I was sick enough to stop at a hospital emergency room and try to get help, but I couldn't speak Spanish and explain my problem. I tried to motion to the young doctors where my problem was by pointing to my stomach and grimacing at the same time. They offered me a bottle of mineral water, suggesting that would be the treatment for stomachaches. I left, and after a few hours of driving, I was so sick, I had to stop on the side of the road. I fell asleep sitting up against a tree. Suddenly I was awakened by a terrible cramp in my belly. Foolishly, I thought it was gas, but to my surprise, an explosion of liquid stool poured out. I was on a country road, several miles away from any town, so I had to get back on my motorcycle, sit on my shit-soaked pants, and drive around until I found a place to stop and clean up. Luckily, a few miles up the road, I saw a campground with showers and bathroom facilities, which is where I was able to clean up.

After that I continued on toward Barcelona but had to stay overnight at a cheap boarding house. The boarding house had three rooms, each with a sink, but only one bathroom to share which was located down the hallway. While I was in my room the cramps were getting worse, when suddenly I had the uncontrollable urge to defecate. I ran to the bathroom in the hallway, but someone was already in there. I ran back to my room, quickly pushed the night table next to the sink, stood up on it and squatted over the sink. Immediately, a stream of liquid stool poured out and went down the drain. The next day I drove off and eventually arrived in Barcelona where I found a youth hostel to stay in. I was so dehydrated by then, having nothing to eat or drink for the last 2 days. I became much sicker, with excruciating belly pain, fever, and diarrhea that consisted of blood and mucus. I couldn't eat and hardly drank anything but sips of water and got weaker each day. Because I didn't speak Spanish, I couldn't explain my problem and didn't know how to ask for help. I became hopeless and didn't care if I died, just so that the pain would stop. I didn't know anything about American Embassies, where Americans could ask for help. I was thinking about writing a farewell letter to my parents, telling them goodbye.

After about seven days there was no more diarrhea because there was nothing left in me, but the PAIN persisted. That's when I found a person working in the youth hostel that spoke a little English and asked them where I could find a doctor. They said that there was a doctor's office about four or five blocks away. Although I had a motorcycle, I was too weak to kick start and ride it, so I slowly shuffled in the direction of the doctor's office. I finally reached the office identified by the universal medical symbol, the caduceus, on his door. I went up and knocked, but no one answered, so I knocked several more times. Apparently, there was a sign stating that the office was closed, but I couldn't read Spanish. I knocked again, and finally he opened the door, looking annoyed, shaking his head *no*, and tried to close the door. I was desperate, so I put my foot inside blocking him from closing it. I couldn't explain my problem in Spanish, so I played charades pointing to my wrist and made a motion as if to cut it, by slashing across it with my fingers. Simultaneously, I made a sound as if blood were gushing out, then pointed to my butt and made the same sound. I didn't know how else to explain it, but thank God he understood. He directed me into his office, then took my blood pressure, listened to my heart and lungs, and palpated my abdomen. He couldn't explain what he thought my problem was, but he seemed to know and wrote out a prescription. He charged me $2.50 for the visit, which I gladly paid. I immediately went to the pharmacy and got the prescription filled. At least now I had hope of getting better, and I returned to the youth hostel. I opened the bottle of pills, which looked like Alka Seltzer tablets—big, round, about the size of a quarter. I couldn't understand the directions because they were in Spanish, so I swallowed one with a sip of water. The tablet wouldn't go down because it was too big, and my throat was so dry. Now, distracted from the belly pain, my attention was focused on my throat, which felt like I swallowed acid. The burning sensation lasted throughout most of the night, but by morning I was able to drink some water.

Gradually, over the next few days, I started to feel better and had a voracious appetite for sugary foods. For the next three days, I ate only cake and cookies. Finally, I had enough strength to get back on my motorcycle, head north through the Pyrenees, and back to France. Eventually I had my first solid bowel movement—"Thank God."

I went on to France, then northern Italy, where I anticipated eating authentic Italian food. Unfortunately, I arrived around 1:00 in the afternoon when the siesta started and had to wait about two hours to get something to eat.

I traveled to the cities of Turin and Milan, and in one of those cities I had my bath towel stolen.

A noteworthy memory was driving through the Italian Alps at about 70 miles per hour, and other motorcyclists on enormous Moto Guzzis whizzing by me. While heading through the Alps, I stopped at a small roadside restaurant that was attached to the owner's house. It was simple, with only a few tables, but the cooking smelled delicious. I couldn't read the menu written in Italian, so I pointed to a random selection. When I was served pasta covered in green sauce, I was appalled. It smelled good, but looked bad, until I tasted it. The green sauce was unbelievably delicious, unlike any Italian food that I had tasted before. The meal consisted of pasta, a salad, bread, and a bottle of mineral water.

I'm not exactly sure, but I think that the meal only cost about a dollar.

After Italy, I went to Switzerland, relieved that I could freely speak English to almost everyone. Up until this time, with the exception of the United Kingdom, I had traveled through non-English-speaking countries. As much as a relief it was to communicate in English, I wasn't prepared for the cold temperature in the Swiss Alps. As I drove higher, the temperature dropped lower. I was so cold that I thought of boarding a train for the remainder of the trip through Switzerland. I was debating whether I should endure another day traveling by motorcycle. After spending a night warming up in a youth hostel tucked high in the Alps, I decided the next morning to make a rapid descent to warmer temperatures. I didn't stay in Switzerland for long, because I was uncomfortable riding my motorcycle, whipped by the cold mountain air.

Going north, I headed for Germany where, again, I was delighted to be around people who spoke English. The cities were modern, and the roads well-maintained, especially the Autobahn, a remarkable example of highway engineering. I remember driving my motorcycle at about 70 miles per hour, when suddenly I was squeezed over towards the right lane by Mercedes and BMWs zipping by.

I noticed that the younger Germans were fluent in English, but the older ones only spoke German and were unfriendly towards Americans. Nothing else really stands out about my travels through Germany.

Next, I headed up to Belgium and made sure I saw Brussels, the capital. I don't remember much about Belgium except that they spoke three different languages, French, German, and Dutch.

After Belgium, I rode on to Holland and headed to Amsterdam, where the liberal laws allowed the use of drugs. Heroin addicts were able to get their drug in a government supervised clinic, and marijuana was smoked freely in the parks. The famous "needle park" had hippies from all over Europe camped out in tents and vans. I stayed overnight in a tent there and got to meet some really weird people. What stood out as the most interesting was Amsterdam's medieval architecture and narrow streets. The buildings were ornate with tall, steepled roofs

The Scandinavian countries were the best, where mostly every young person was fluent in English. The youth hostels were the cleanest, and the women, blond and blue-eyed, were beautiful. In contrast, I must have stood out, being Italian—tan, with curly, dark-brown hair.

Denmark was the first Scandinavian country that I visited. The big attraction was Tivoli Gardens, an amusement park in the city of Copenhagen. The city had buildings from the 1600's, quaint, and the setting for stories from Hans Christian Anderson. I remember walking down a narrow street, in a district known for its drug trade, when a big Danish guy with a red beard approached me. He looked like a Viking and asked me if I was looking to buy pot or acid. I bought mescaline thinking that it was a natural hallucinogen used in American Indian religious ceremonies. Later that night, I found a youth hostel which consisted of large, old army tents that slept about sixteen people. There weren't any beds, so we slept on the ground in sleeping bags. The cost of a one-night stay, including breakfast, was only a dollar. The manager was a pretty, young Danish girl named Jutta, whom I met as soon as I arrived. As the day went on, we had the chance to talk about important world issues and the American involvement in Viet Nam. Later that day, she invited me to go with her to meet some friends. We rode on my motorcycle through the city of Copenhagen to her friend's apartment. She introduced me, then said that she wanted me to tell her friends the story about how

I enlisted in the Air Force and later decided to leave. The younger generation throughout Europe were naturally antiwar, especially after their parents experienced it first-hand. They were impressed that young Americans like myself were back home protesting against the war, and they were intrigued by my story and how I had a change of heart.

My next stop was Sweden, but first I had to take a ferry across the North Sea from Denmark.

After I arrived in Sweden, I headed through beautiful countryside, visiting ancient castles and historic sites. One site in particular had relics of a Viking civilization, thousands of years old. There were rock carvings with inscriptions over two thousand years old, and Viking burial grounds with stone monuments that were over three thousand years old. Driving farther north, I eventually arrived in Stockholm where I looked for the youth hostel, but instead of a building, there was an old ship, seventy-five years old or more, converted into a youth hostel. It was a large ship permanently anchored in the harbor across from the King's Palace.

When I arrived, I couldn't get in to register because the entrance to the hostel was closed. The manager, a tall blond girl, was just leaving for lunch. She explained that she had to leave so she could catch the bus. When I said that I would take her home on my motorcycle, she readily agreed. Her name was Leanae, and we rode together to the apartment building where she lived with her father. She invited me in and showed me an interesting collection that was once her grandfather's. He was a world traveler and collected objects from different countries. I remember seeing preserved tarantulas, exotic butterflies, and some fossilized seashells. I thought her grandfather must have been cool, traveling to all those different countries collecting objects that had a special significance. I waited for Leanae to eat lunch, then drove her back to the youth hostel. The ship's bunks were below deck, as well as a galley where the travelers could prepare their own food. There were also open areas with communal showers and toilets down below deck.

There were so many pretty girls in Sweden, but one stood out from the rest. While I was shopping in a supermarket looking for peanut butter, I noticed several butchers cutting meat. One was a girl about twenty years old and very beautiful. When I couldn't find peanut butter and didn't know what it was called in Swedish, I looked around for someone to ask. That's when I decided to ask that beautiful girl cutting meat. She was friendly, understood English, and realized it was peanut butter that I was looking for. She walked me over to the right shelf and handed me a jar of peanut butter. I thanked her and then asked her what she was doing cutting meat, because she was so beautiful, and she should be in magazines. I wasn't surprised when she told me that she was a "module," and they took pictures of her. So, I was right, she was a model, and too beautiful to be just a butcher. Before I left, she gave me her phone number and said she wanted to take me out to dinner. I found out it was customary for Swedish women to sometimes pay for their date's dinner. The next day I met her, and we drove off on my motorcycle to a restaurant that she was familiar with. After we ate, she brought me to her cabin in the country where she played the guitar and sang *Where Have All the Flowers Gone*, by Peter, Paul, and Mary, to me. Whenever I hear that song, I'm reminded of that day with that beautiful Swedish girl singing. I can't believe that I didn't keep in touch with that girl, so beautiful and talented. I think it was because I had a lot of traveling to do, and more girls to meet, just like the song, *The Wanderer*.

While I was in Stockholm, I saw another amazing artifact from the Viking era in a museum in Stockholm. It was an old ship, buried for centuries under the mud in a canal in Stockholm. It was on display under a constant mist of a chemical solution to preserve it. More interesting was the story about how it was discovered, buried under the canal for centuries. The story tells about a fisherman, who for years rowed his boat up and down the canal looking for the lost ship.

Supposedly, he had chains with hooks attached so that he could snag anything buried in the mud. Finally, in the late 1960's, he hooked on to something as he was rowing. After convincing the authorities of his finding, the ship was discovered and carefully removed from the bottom of the canal.

I spent more time in Sweden than most other countries because of the beautiful girls. Finally, the night before I left, I wanted to say goodbye to Leanae, the manager of the youth hostel. She wasn't working that night, so I wouldn't see her again before I left in the morning. It was sad to leave and never say goodbye, so I decided to try and find her apartment somewhere in the big city of Stockholm. I rode through the city trying to remember the streets that she had pointed out when I drove her home the first day. Luckily, I found the street, but the apartment buildings looked the same, so I chose the one that I thought was hers. I remembered that her apartment was on about the fifth or sixth floor, so I stood on the sidewalk and shouted up her name several times, until finally her father stuck his head out the window. He shouted down in English that she went out to a disco club with her friends. I shouted back up, asking him to tell her that George, the American, was leaving in the morning and said goodbye. I drove back to the youth hostel, sad, but at least I was able to tell her father to give her the message that I wanted to say goodbye.

That night I went to sleep earlier than usual. About 1:00 a.m., I was suddenly awakened by someone gently shaking me. It was Leanae, who said when she got the message from her father, she had to see me again. She whispered something like, "I never wanted anything more in my life, than to see you again."

We couldn't talk much because the other travelers were sleeping in the bunk beds next to me.

She said follow me, then led me out of the sleeping area below deck and up to the top of the ship. On the top deck was the captain's quarters, off-limits and maintained as a museum. Inside there were old nautical instruments, a captain's log book, and his sleeping quarters. Leanae was the manager, so she had the key, and we both went in. There we had privacy and tried not to rock the ship.

Norway was next on the list. It was to the west of Sweden, reached by rural roads through beautiful mountains covered in pine. The weather was nice, with the sun shining and warm mountain breezes tickling my face. I eventually reached the capital, Oslo, but I don't remember much except the ride on the way in.

The last Scandinavian country on my list was Finland, which was far to the east, across the Baltic Sea. I left Norway, then drove back across Sweden until I reached Stockholm. Just outside the city, I boarded a ship and stored my motorcycle down below deck. Then we headed out to Helsinki, which was across the Baltic Sea. The ship had a restaurant that was serving a buffet-style Swedish smorgasbord. It looked delicious, especially because I hadn't eaten in a restaurant in almost a month. I couldn't afford it, so I snuck in line, and stuffed myself, by sampling everything. I really enjoyed it, but not for long. As the ship started rocking on the rough Baltic Sea, I started to become nauseous. It wasn't more than fifteen minutes after I had finished eating that I had to run to the men's room and throw up. It was such a waste of the first large meal that I had eaten. Up until that time, I had eaten only cheese, bread, apples, a little meat, and sometimes, peanut butter sandwiches.

The ship finally arrived at a port in Helsinki, the capital of Finland. Like most of the other places that I had visited, I didn't know much about it. I found out that Helsinki hosted the 1968 Olympics, and it was only about five hundred miles from Russia. I thought about getting a visa so that I could visit Russia, but I changed my mind because the process would take too long.

Of all the Scandinavian countries, Finland was the poorest, and the people were not as sophisticated as the other countries. Only a few spoke English, alcoholism was common, and the people were sloppy in their dress. My main objective in Finland was to go up to the Arctic Circle, which was several hours north of Helsinki. I was advised not to drive my motorcycle all the way up to Rovaniemi, the nearest town in the Arctic Circle, so, instead, I took a train part of the way. Many of the people appeared to be poor Laplanders with coarse Eurasian facial features. Instead of suitcases, they had their belongings wrapped in a bundle made from blankets. At the train station there was a disheveled man standing up on a platform, who, at first glance, appeared to be rolling something in his hands. That's when I noticed a few women staring at the man with shocked looks on their faces. As I looked closer, I realized that the man was masturbating in front of everybody.

Finally, I boarded the train to the Arctic Circle, which was about 400 miles north of Helsinki. It was jammed with Laplanders carrying their bundles, many standing or sitting on the floor because of the lack of seats available. During the train trip, I could see why I was advised not to ride my motorcycle, because the landscape was austere and barely populated. Finally, we arrived, and as soon as I got off the train, I took a picture of the official sign designating we were at the Arctic Circle. The sign was in about five different languages, and seeing it was worth the trip. Because of the latitude, during the summer, daylight was visible 24 hours a day. Although it faded by midnight it was still bright enough to read the newspaper throughout the night.

I visited historical sites where there were remnants of sod-covered log huts, half-buried underground. They were constructed from the most basic materials, providing shelter against the harsh arctic winters.

The people made their living herding reindeer, and to see them dressed in their traditional work clothes made it look like time stood still.

Finland was the northernmost Scandinavian country I visited, and now it was time to head south, backtracking through Europe, heading toward the French coastal city of Calais. I had already been on the road for two months, and now I was going back across the English Channel to finish my tour of Great Britain. I got off the ferry at Dover, England (the White Cliffs of Dover), and headed north through England, finally reaching Scotland.

Edinburgh, the capital of Scotland, was my main goal. It was one of the oldest cities in Europe and noted for the famous Edinburgh Castle. It was one of the oldest fortified castles in Europe, and it dominates the skyline. It houses Scotland's Crown Jewels and still serves as a military headquarters. I was getting low on money while I was there, so I slept outside under an overhang the first night and on the floor in a bus station the next night.

After Scotland, I headed back south to England in a southwest direction, passing through Liverpool, to finally reach the country of Wales. I don't remember anything about Wales, except that's where I took the ferry to cross the Irish Sea to Ireland. We docked in Dublin, and off I went, riding my motorcycle through the Irish countryside. I can't remember anything special about Ireland, and after a few days, sailed back across the Irish Sea to England.

My trip from North Africa to the Arctic Circle was finally coming to an end. I had spent two-and- a-half months riding my motorcycle, traveling almost nine thousand miles through deserts and mountains. I managed to do that on less than two dollars a day. I started out knowing little about Europe, and now was empowered by the experience of seeing different countries and their respective cultures. All the time that I was traveling, my only communication back home was by postcards. My parents had no idea of my itinerary or my whereabouts because the postcards took about ten days to reach them.

August 1971: Returning from Europe

I flew back to New York, tired after an eight-hour flight, and then had to take two buses to get to my home in New Jersey. My parents had no idea when I would come home, so I wanted to surprise them. I expected my father to be proud of me, and excited that I was home, safe and sound. As I walked into the house my father was sitting at the kitchen table. I had a big smile on my face and thought that he would jump up and hug me, but he just sat there. I felt disappointed that he didn't seem excited to see me after being gone so long. Didn't he want to hear about the countries that I visited, and the people I met? Apparently not, because all he said was that he was glad that I made it home alright. I don't think that he realized that my world was turned upside down after experiencing the adventure of a lifetime. Now I knew what was out there: a much bigger world with unlimited possibilities.

In addition to my trip to Europe, reading extensively had been the galvanizing force that opened my mind. Between the ages of nineteen and twenty-one, I had read so much that my dictionary was falling apart from looking up so many words. Eventually, I had to duct tape the binding to keep it together. I wrote down every word that I didn't know, along with its definition, and kept the list as a reminder of my determination to learn.

College, Age 21

When I returned from Europe, I felt enriched, transformed by the experience into a new person with unlimited potential to explore the world like never before. I thought about what my old friend Bobby Geddis said: "Georgie, you've gotta see the world." Now I knew why he encouraged me, so that I would realize my potential and escape the routine existence that would have limited my growth. I remembered that before I decided to go to Europe, I told my fellow carpenter coworkers that I would be back in a few months. Now that

I returned, I stopped by my old job to tell my coworkers goodbye and that I wasn't returning to carpentry. I told them that my trip through Europe opened my eyes to a bigger world and proudly announced that I was going to start college in the fall.

That fall I enrolled at Fairleigh Dickinson University in Rutherford, New Jersey. Not knowing what career to choose, I chose a liberal arts curriculum. After a few months, I thought about becoming a teacher and finished two semesters with a B average. My plans to start the second year as an education major came to an abrupt halt when I discovered that no teaching jobs were available. This was because anyone trying to avoid the draft took advantage of the deferments given to teachers during the Vietnam War. I didn't want to spend another three years going to college and not find a job. I would be better off staying with carpentry, but I liked the academic atmosphere and intellectual stimulation that college gave me. I didn't mind spending extra years in college if I could find a career that I liked and a guarantee that I could get a job after graduation. The first choices that came to mind were doctor, dentist, and lawyer. I thought to myself, *wait a minute, becoming a doctor, wasn't that my dream when I was eight years old and asked for that Johnson & Johnson first aid kit for Christmas? Why not give it a try?* Enthusiastic, I naively decided to switch my major and enrolled in a pre-med curriculum at Rutgers University in Newark, New Jersey.

Ironically some of my classes were scheduled in the same building that I had worked on as a carpenter a few years before. I was enthusiastic to begin learning about the science courses preparing me for the rigorous studies required in medical school. I went to my local library to look up the American Medical Association pamphlet for students planning on going to medical school. I was intimidated by the names of some of the advanced courses that were suggested for entry into medical school. More alarming was the mention that a student needed to obtain at least a B+, or preferably an A average as proof that they would be able to endure the rigorous curriculum pursuing a medical degree. That was more demanding than I had imagined, but I tried to be optimistic, hoping that my enthusiasm would be enough to meet the challenge. After all, I was able to earn a B average in the liberal arts curriculum the first year, and although pre-med would be more challenging, I would study longer and harder. So, off I went to Rutgers University, excited to be enrolled as a sophomore in the pre-med curriculum. Within the first week I knew that something was wrong—very wrong. I didn't know how to solve chemistry problems that involved decimals and fractions because I never took chemistry in high school, and nothing more than basic math. It was like a foreign language to me, with terms like *ratio*, *proportion, numerator,* and *denominator*. A simple problem adding decimals overwhelmed me. It was pathetic that I couldn't add $1 + 1.1 = 2.1$. Trying to add fractions was just as confusing. The example, $\frac{1}{4} + \frac{3}{4} = 1$, didn't make sense, because when I added $\frac{1}{4} + 3/4$, it equaled $4/4$, not 1. After a few weeks of humiliation, frustration, and a shattered dream, I quit college.

Embarrassed, I returned to the union carpentry job that I had left the year before and surprised my co-workers, who asked me what happened to my plans of becoming a doctor. I explained what happened and how difficult the pre-med courses were. Sympathetically, and with good intentions, they tried to protect my pride by saying that they knew how difficult it was to become a doctor, and that a person had to be really smart.

They tried to humor me, saying, "Don't worry, kid, at least with carpentry you can always make a good living."

So, this was my destiny, I thought, as I returned to my old job as a carpenter.

***

It was a miserable grey October day, wet, and cold, and I was assigned to carry heavy planks through ankle deep mud that almost sucked my boots off. I continued working, my spirit broken, and my pride stripped away, often wondering if I dropped out because I wasn't smart enough, or was it due to my lack of education. I thought if only I could go back to high school, I wouldn't mind doing 4 years over again, and this time I wouldn't waste it. Although that wasn't possible, over the next several months I tried to figure out a way to learn the math and science that I missed in high school.

Eventually I found out there were night courses in math and chemistry taught on the high school level, so maybe there was a chance that I could learn enough to return to a pre-med program. Once again, I was hopeful, even though it had been six months since dropping out of college, my dreams still outweighed my fears.

My first night course was a review of algebra, but it was way over my head because I never learned the basics. I didn't know enough to review, so I shamefully dropped out, trying to reassure myself that I wasn't stupid—it was a lack of education. I realized that I needed a basic math course, not a review; but how basic...I wasn't sure. Well, I soon found out the answer.

I heard that there was a private education center in Montclair, New Jersey, that tutored students who needed help to boost their grades. At the education center, I inquired if I could enroll in a basic math course in order to prepare for a pre-med curriculum. The teacher was surprised to see an adult interested in his school, which only provided teaching on the elementary level. He was very understanding and said that they didn't have an adult program, but he would give me their 8th grade math test to see where my weakness was. When I finished the test, he immediately graded it and said, "You failed the 8th grade math test."

I felt like I was hit in the head with a sledgehammer. Driving home from there I was devastated beyond belief, convinced that I was a fool to even think that I was smart enough to become a doctor. Now, without a doubt, this proved how dumb I really was. I felt mentally castrated, hopeless not only to pursue a medical career, but to even manage my life in general. I was a loser—let's face it, failing an elementary school math test at 22 years old. I was tormented and tried not to allow myself to think that I was stupid, struggling to believe it was my lack of education, not my lack of intelligence. I was heartbroken and kept thinking, *if only I could have paid attention in high school, I would have had a chance, but now it's too late.* But then I remembered back when I was seventeen, the two rules to live by. The first was, "I can't be beat until I'm down and out and can't get up." The second: "When I grow older and look back, I'll never say *I wished it were,* or *wished it could have been.* I'll do it now and either succeed or fail."

I was haunted by imagining the future—my life unfulfilled, and being left wondering, *what if I hadn't given up, and I finally had became a doctor?* I had to keep trying, realizing that failure isn't the end of the road, but only a stop along the way—guiding you over the hills and around the bends, leading you to your final destination.

I used that philosophy to get back on my feet again and began searching for basic math and chemistry courses. Finally, I found a basic math course, hoping that this time it would emphasize the fundamentals so that I would have a foundation to build upon. There was also a chemistry course offered on the same basic level, so I enrolled in it. There was one more subject that I needed—physics— but there were no courses available. Even if I learned math and chemistry, I wouldn't be prepared to pursue a pre-med curriculum without physics. I was up against a wall, desperate to learn physics. It was a long shot when I decided to go back to my old Catholic high school and ask the principal if I could audit the sophomore physics class. The principal, a Nun, said that she would give me permission to audit the sophomore physics class, but I had to wear the Catholic school attire consisting of a white shirt, tie, and sport jacket. I was hopeful again now that I had the opportunity to learn chemistry, and by this time, shame and failure no longer mattered; I couldn't go any further down. Now, all that I had left was determination and perseverance to pull me through, so at age twenty-two I was going to class with 15-year-old sophomore students. Before I started the class, I spoke to the physics teacher and explained my situation. He told me that he understood and confessed that he had wanted to go to medical school, but it took too many years. Next, I needed the physics book provided by the school, and went to the book storage room to sign it out. However, I didn't know that there were specific times posted stating when the storage room would be open. I saw an intercom adjacent to the door, pushed the call button, and heard someone answer. I said that I needed a book. There was no reply, but a minute later a nun came flying around the corner and reprimanded me for disturbing her. She pointed to the sign showing the times that the book storage was open. It was déjà vu, just like I remembered getting yelled at in high school for screwing up. I apologized, saying that I didn't see the times posted. The next day that same nun came looking for me and said, "I'm so sorry, Mr. Castellano, I thought that you were one of the sophomore students." I told her she didn't need to apologize because this was my only opportunity to learn physics, and besides, I felt at home in my old high school being reprimanded by nuns.

The same year, still twenty-two years old, I occasionally needed a break from all the remedial courses, so I went on short trips to Maine and Florida. One of those trips was when I was asked to drive my grandmother's car to Florida. I made it in a little over 24 hours and stayed a few days visiting with my Uncle Junior. I wanted some adventure, and instead of flying home, I decided to hitchhike back to New Jersey. I started out with a knapsack on my back and walked over to stand on the shoulder of Interstate 95 going north. It wasn't long before a beat-up old car with Alabama plates pulled over. When I saw the driver, who looked like Charles Mason, with long hair and a shaggy beard, I had second thoughts about getting in. As soon as I got in the guy asked, "You got a license, man? Because I don't."

I said *yes*, but thought, *what the hell did I get myself mixed up in?*

He said, "You've got to drive because I don't want to get in trouble." Then he asked how far I was going, and I told him New Jersey. He said he was going to Maryland and wanted me to eventually take over the driving. I wasn't sure if I wanted to stay with this guy because if he's in trouble, I did not want to be involved. He looked nervous, constantly looking out for cops and repeatedly saying that I had to drive. Then, suddenly, he panicked and slowed down when he saw a state trooper parked on the side of the highway. He made it obvious, by slowing down, that he was being extra cautious, which attracted that trooper's attention. He watched as the trooper sped up onto the highway behind us, and he shouted, "He's coming after us!"

He jumped over towards me, pulling me out of the seat so that I could take the wheel. I said, "No!" and pushed him back, but he wouldn't budge. I finally shuffled over and started driving. This was taking place at 55 miles per hour with the trooper two car-lengths behind us. The trooper then sped by us, and about two miles down the road, he was waiting and pulled us over. I thought, *Holy shit, what did this guy do?*

The trooper came up to the driver's side of the car and told me to get out and the other guy to stay in. He looked at my license, then called in to headquarters, and after a few minutes, he said that I was wanted in Miami for bank robbery. In the meantime, another trooper sped up and jumped out and told me to stand next to his car with my hands on the hood.

I said, "I'll stand there, but I'm going to turn and face the sun, after all I came to Florida to get a tan."

While the first trooper was questioning the other guy, the other one asked what I was doing in Florida. I said that I was visiting my uncle in Orlando. Then he asked my uncle's name, which I refused to give him because my uncle was a well-known gangster and that could have triggered a further investigation.

Finally, the first trooper came back to me and said, "I know that the other guy is the owner of the car and drove without a license from Alabama, but I didn't see him driving so I can't arrest him." Then he said, "You have to drive him home all the way to Maryland."

I said *okay* because I was going to Jersey anyway. When I got back in the car I said, "I thought you did something really bad, and I was going to get in trouble too."

He said that he thought the same about me. Then he said that the car was his brother's, who was in jail in Alabama, and he was driving it home to Maryland for him. The reason he didn't have a license was because he was driving a pickup truck overloaded with firewood, was given a fine, and couldn't afford to pay it. As we drove north, I decided to stop at a Howard Johnson's restaurant to get something to eat. He said that he didn't have enough money to eat, just enough for gas. It was an "all you can eat" buffet, so I ate a lot while he sat and watched. When I finished, I asked him what he wanted to eat, then went back up, filled the plate, and brought it back to him. Many hours later we finally made it to Maryland, where I got out and started hitchhiking the rest of the way to New Jersey.

For the next year I attended night classes in math and chemistry, while auditing physics class during the day. After that year I felt more confident, but with apprehension, decided to enter a pre-med program at a different college, William Paterson College in Wayne, New Jersey. This would be my third college, but it wouldn't be my last. As a pre-med student, pre-calculus was a required course, and although the name was scary, it was only algebra. My first test didn't seem too difficult, but I only got a C and couldn't believe that after a year of math review, I still wasn't able to do well. I needed to maintain a B+ average in my courses in order to get accepted into med school, and with a C in math, it would be almost impossible. Desperate, I went to the math professor and asked if I got an A on every test the rest of the semester, would he drop my lowest grade of C. He said that he had never done that before, and it would be unlikely that I would get an A on every test the rest of the semester because they would become more difficult as the year progressed. He finally agreed, but he still doubted it would be possible. With that little spark of hope, I immediately set out to find a tutor. I hired a student who was a junior majoring in math. He taught me algebra four or five days a week, assisted by my $75.00 Texas Instruments calculator. I got an A on the next test. Now I was determined and more confident, pushing myself week after week with tutored lessons, and eventually got an A on all the remaining tests. The professor was amazed and said that he would gladly give me a well-deserved A for the course.

I enrolled in the other required pre-med courses during my sophomore year at William Paterson College, except for the first half of organic chemistry. I decided to take it at my old college, Fairleigh Dickinson, in Rutherford, New Jersey. The reason was simply because I knew that the course would be less intense and that earning an A or B wouldn't be as difficult. By the end of my sophomore year, I was able to manage a B+ average in the pre-med courses, including the first half of organic chemistry. I was prepared to start my third year of college at age twenty-three but still had to complete two more years of pre-med. That meant that I would be twenty-five years old by the time of college graduation and then would still have four years of medical school before I would become a doctor.

After that I would still have to complete between three to five years of residency, depending on the field that I chose. I was getting impatient when I realized I would be at least thirty-five years old before I would be able to practice as a doctor. It was at that time that I saw an ad, in the *New York Times*, for a new foreign medical school located in the Dominican Republic that only required three years of college to enter. That would eliminate taking another year of pre-med and allow me to graduate a year sooner. I checked out the school's credentials and found out it was approved by the World Health Organization, a requirement needed to practice medicine in the United States. The main drawback was that all the courses were taught in Spanish, which I knew would be a challenge. I decided to go to New York City for an interview, was accepted soon after, and sent in my $3,000 deposit. At that time, I didn't know where the Dominican Republic was located nor anything about the living conditions there. I learned that it was hot, requiring light-weight clothing, so I foolishly bought two pairs of polyester pants, thinking that they would be cool and breathable—big mistake! I was foolish and didn't research the living conditions, culture, or type of government. When I arrived at the airport in Santo Domingo, the capital of the Dominican Republic, I was shocked to see the poverty just outside the city. Besides that, there were machine gun-wielding soldiers, along the roads, guarding major businesses and public buildings. The roads outside the city were horrible, especially those on the route to San Pedro de Marcoris, the town where the medical school was located. The taxi driver spoke little English while driving me over unpaved, dusty roads, showing me the dilapidated shacks where the people lived. There were almost no modern buildings or stores, except for an old factory where they processed molasses from sugar cane. As we drove through the town, down one of the hot dusty streets, the taxi driver pointed out a man standing on the front porch of his run-down house with his shirt unbuttoned and a big belly hanging out. He must have been an important man because the taxi driver knew who he was and said, "That man is the professor of anatomy at the medical school in the city."

That was just the beginning of the cultural shock that I was to encounter in the coming weeks. The taxi driver dropped me off in front of the only hotel in the town. I got out with my backpack and suitcase and entered the hotel. I couldn't afford a room there, and only stopped to get information about available housing. I found living accommodations in an old private school that was divided up into separate unfurnished rooms. There was absolutely no furniture, so I had to sleep on the tile floor with my clothing underneath me to keep out the cold. The bathroom was outside in a separate building and had an inch of water flooding the floor, the result of a leaky pipe. Any cooking had to be done outside on a grill using charcoal or wood for fuel. As miserable as conditions were, I willingly accepted the uncomfortable living conditions because my dream of becoming a doctor was worth the sacrifice. After living there for about a week, I heard of a two- bedroom house for rent that I could share with another medical student. I met the other American student, a guy named Wally, who was already living there. I moved into the sparsely furnished two-bedroom house and had my own bedroom. There was a bed, but no bed linens, and one pillow that smelled awful. At least it was more livable than the first place that I had stayed.

My next move was to contact the medical school representative and start the Spanish classes scheduled to begin one month prior to starting school. I doubted that would be enough time to become fluent enough in Spanish to handle medical school. Worse yet, I found out that the school had not been built yet, but only existed on paper. It was true that it was a legitimate school approved by the World Health Organization, but it had no physical plant, and classes were to be held in various private homes and community buildings. I started to become doubtful of the legitimacy of this new school which further strained my optimism. Day by day, I was appalled by the squalid living conditions and emaciated people walking around barefoot. Even the pigs were almost unrecognizable with their ribs sticking out because there was no garbage to eat. The open-air markets were dirty with very few canned goods or prepackaged food. Most of the items were sold loosely, like beans and rice scooped into bags, fly-covered meat wrapped in brown paper, and unrefrigerated dairy products. I really tried to remain hopeful, but gradually started to doubt that I would ever earn a medical degree in this country. Finally, the straw that broke the camel's back was when I found that a year of social service, sometimes in a leper colony, was required after graduating medical school. That was enough, with the deplorable living conditions, only one month of Spanish before school started, and no actual medical school building. I decided to leave.

With my dream shattered again, and my life savings of $3,000 gone, I booked a flight on a propeller plane to Puerto Rico and from there I flew to JFK airport in New York. To get home to New Jersey I had to take several buses and finally was dropped off a few blocks from my house. Lugging my suitcase and backpack, I entered my house, surprising my parents who had no idea that I was coming home. When I entered my house, I'll never forget the look of disappointment on my father's face. He said that he told his fellow carpenters that his son was going to medical school, but now he was embarrassed to tell them that I quit. I explained the reason for leaving, the deplorable living conditions, the school not yet built, and a year of social service after graduation. I was humiliated and sad to have let my father down, but worse, it was the end of my dream of ever becoming a doctor. My father's disappointment was obvious, but he said that he would ask his boss if I could work on the same construction job with him. Humiliated and dejected, I returned to my union carpentry job for the SECOND time. When my coworkers asked what happened this time, I tried to justify leaving medical school because of the uncertainty of the program and the horrible living conditions.

Around age twenty-four, I went down to the Jersey shore for the weekend and stopped at a local bar. I was surprised when I met an old college classmate Frank, who helped me in freshman year to pass algebra. I remembered him telling me that he wanted to go into demolition, the type that collapses buildings in urban settings. That was three years ago, and at that time, I wanted to become a teacher, never entertaining the idea of becoming a doctor. I had lost contact with him until I met up with him at the bar, where he introduced me to his girlfriend Judy. She was very friendly, and I was flattered that she had heard about me from Frank's college days. During the conversation she mentioned how impressed she was hearing about Frank and me riding our motorcycles through Europe and North Africa. I was caught off guard, not knowing what to say when she started to ask me questions about it. I hesitated to answer and tried to cover up the fact that I went alone. I tried to change the subject, but I know that she caught on, and she just rolled her eyes. I felt bad for Frank, thinking that he wanted to impress his girlfriend by inserting himself into my adventure that I shared with him during freshman year. At that time, I didn't think that the trip was that big of a deal and even forgot that I had told him about it.

I was finally free of my unrealistic dream of becoming a doctor, and after several months working in construction, I decided to go up to Bangor, Maine. I had no particular plans in mind but just wanted to experience new surroundings. I rented a room in a boarding house and then checked the newspaper for available jobs. One ad caught my eye: *Looking for a laborer to help build a stone house.*

I answered the ad and was hired by the yuppie couple that was trying to live off the grid. The construction utilized the slip-form method, which consisted of a form filled with randomly gathered field stones embedded in cement. After the cement dried, the form was separated from the one below it and raised up to the next level. Although the material was inexpensive, the process was labor-intensive, which helped me forget my failed attempt at medical school. While living in Bangor, I sometimes walked downtown, and one day I happened to pass a bookstore and noticed some books on display in the window. One stood out from the rest, titled *The Big Little World of Doc Pritham*. I went in to check it out, leafed through the pages, and eagerly bought it. *Wow*, I thought as I read it, *a country doctor that lived a life like I imagined when I was 8 years old and asked for the Johnson & Johnson General First Aid Kit.* I probably finished reading that book in a day or two and was excited to discover that the author, Dorothy Clark Wilson, lived just outside of Bangor, in Orono, Maine. It was amazing, not only to read about a doctor who did as I had once dreamed of doing, but the author living close by too. I looked up the author's name in the phone book and hesitantly called the number. She answered, and I told her that I had just finished reading the book about Doc Pritham and that I would really like to talk to her. Politely, she said *yes* and invited me to her house. I was so excited and asked if I could come right then. She said sure and proceeded to give me directions. I drove over right away and met her and her husband who, I discovered, were both missionaries who had traveled around the world. She had written over a dozen books. The latest one was the one about Doc Pritham. She said that the doctor was a legend up in Greenville, Maine, practicing until he was 92 years old. He had his office in his house for over 50 years and traveled to remote areas in all kinds of weather, using any means of transportation necessary, to reach lumber camps or isolated cabins way up north. He traveled on snowshoes, in boats, on trains, and even converted a car into an all-terrain vehicle with caterpillar tracks instead of wheels. She said that Doc Pritham was a very private person, and the only reason that he would let her write about his life was to encourage young doctors to practice in rural areas. Although he died a few years prior to our meeting, at age 95, she said that his wife Sadie was still alive and living in the same house where he had his office for over 50 years. All during my visit with the author, Dorothy Clark Wilson, my heart was pounding because I couldn't wait to go up to Greenville, Maine, to meet Doc Pritham's wife and check out the town. During that visit I thanked the author and told her that her book was an inspiration because I had wanted to be a country doctor since I was 8 years old but had sadly given up the idea. Now, I was eager to see, firsthand, the actual setting of this country doctor's practice, like the one that I had imagined when I was eight years old. From Bangor, I drove about 2½ hours north to Greenville, which was a remote town located close to the Canadian border. From reading the book, I recognized many of the buildings and landmarks and eventually found the doctor's house. The house looked exactly like it did when he started his practice 50 years prior. I had to meet his wife so that I could know if what was once a dream for an eight-year-old boy was real—a country doctor making house calls in a rural setting.

Excited, I went up to the house, knocked on the door, and she answered and welcomed me in. She looked just like her picture in the book. She was old but had a clear mind and a good memory. I told her that after I read the book about Doc Pritham, I was so excited that I called the author and visited her and that's when she had told me that Doc Pritham's wife was still living in the same house. It was an inspiration to talk to a country doctor's wife who recounted his experiences over the last 60 years. After my visit with her, I went into the town of Greenville and asked around about the doctor's practice and the legacy that he left behind. Just as I had read in the book, I was told that he was dedicated, traveled anywhere, anytime, and by any means, in order to care for his patients. He often wasn't paid for his services, and over the years the amount of money owed to him would be enough for someone to retire.

That was it! The fire was lit again because now I actually saw first-hand what, years ago, was only in the imagination of an 8-year old—a country doctor practicing in a rural area. There was no stopping me now, but I had to complete the second half of organic chemistry. I enrolled at the University of Maine in Orono, but now two years have passed since I took the first half of organic chemistry, so I had a difficult time starting the second half. I vaguely remembered the molecular configurations and chemical reactions, so after the second week into the course, I dropped out. I knew that it would be difficult to get an A or even a B, and I couldn't afford a grade of C if I wanted to be accepted into medical school. This was the fourth time that I dropped out of college, but I planned on eventually taking the second half during the summer. By this time, I was determined to finish the rest of the pre-med program and decided to return to New Jersey. I returned to my job as a carpenter while I searched for a summer course in organic chemistry. I found out that Jersey City State Teachers College offered part one and part two of organic chemistry during the summer, so I enrolled for the fifth time in a different college. I attended classes two days a week and worked the other three on a construction job. Maybe because summer courses were easier and I had more time to study, I received an A for the second half of organic chemistry. With that weight off my back, I returned to William Paterson College and, over the next two years, took the necessary pre-med courses. During that time, I took the MCATS, a three-part standardized test required by all medical schools. The test is taken by all pre-med students, including the "cream of the crop" students from prestigious schools like Harvard, Princeton, Yale, and Stanford. It was no surprise that I did poorly on the math section, but I scored in the top 2% in verbal and reading comprehension. I realized that math had always been holding me back, but now I was going to focus on my strengths, and not let my weakness get me down. There were two other categories on the test, both of which I received an average score.

Finally, after five years of suffering failure after failure, the humiliation of learning remedial math and science, attending five different colleges, and an aborted attempt at a foreign medical school, I graduated from William Paterson College at age 26.

Now, I was faced with the uncertainty of getting into a New Jersey medical school, knowing that the odds were against me. To get accepted, it was necessary to have a grade point average of at least a B+, or an A, and preferably, participation in a research project. With those high academic standards, I doubted that I would get accepted into a New Jersey medical school. However, my grades were good enough to have been accepted in out-of-state schools, but the tuition was unaffordable to me. Frustrated, I didn't know where to apply, but I heard of a doctor practicing in my area who went to medical school in Italy, and I thought that might be an alternative. I made an appointment at his office as if I had a medical problem. On the scheduled day, I arrived and filled out the customary forms. When the doctor called me in, I immediately told him that I wasn't a patient, but I would pay his fee just to tell me about the process needed to get into an Italian medical school. He smiled and said there would be no charge and that he would be happy to discuss it at a time that would be convenient for both of us. Meanwhile, I discovered that there were other students from New Jersey studying medicine in Mexico, and after four years, they were able to return to the U.S. and enter a residency program. After hearing that, I considered going to Mexico, and I was able to contact a few local students who were already studying medicine there. I inquired about the cost of tuition and the living conditions, but the biggest challenge was that the classes were taught in Spanish.

Now I was hopeful after hearing first-hand that there was an alternative to an American medical school; however, before I could even apply, I had to earn enough money for the application fee, the plane fare, and the first year's tuition. Due to an economic recession at the time, there were few carpenter jobs, so I looked for any work available. I found a job, paying three dollars an hour, working at the local Woolworth's five-and-dime store, sweeping floors and stocking shelves. On occasion, some of my former high school classmates came in to shop, and when they saw me working as a stock boy, they patronizingly said, "We heard that you wanted to be a doctor." With confidence, I said that I planned on going to medical school, but I needed to earn enough money for the application fee and the interview. I could understand my classmates' skepticism—here they were, already married with children and successfully employed, and I was twenty-six years old working for minimum wages.

They probably thought, if I wasn't in med school yet, it was never going to happen.

Besides working at Woolworth's from 9 a.m. to 5 p.m., I had two other jobs. One was from 7 p.m. to 10 p.m., collecting bad checks, and the other was from 11 p.m. to 7 a.m., as a security guard. I was able to work around the clock by taking a folding lawn chair to my security guard job and sleeping in the trailer at the job site until 6 a.m. I made sure that I got up in the morning before the workers arrived. I would go home, take a shower, eat breakfast, and start my job at Woolworth's at 9 a.m. I did this routine for months, trying to earn as much money as I could, in case I was granted an interview at the medical school in Mexico. Because of my work schedule I had little time off and no social life. My ex-girlfriend had already told me, the year before, that she wouldn't wait ten years for me to become a doctor, and with my work schedule I didn't have time to date any girls. The only night that I had a break was Friday because I got off from Woolworth's at 5 p.m. and didn't have to work collecting checks between 7 p.m. and 10 p.m. I had six hours off, but still had to be at my security job at 11 p.m. Lonely for some social interaction, I decided to go to a local nightclub on a Friday night before I had to go to my security job. I went to the club around 8:00 and had about two hours before I had to leave. While I was there, I met a really pretty girl, and we talked for over an hour. Finally, when I had to leave, I asked her for her phone number, but she refused to give it to me. She said if I wanted to see her, she might be back next week. I left the club frustrated and sad because that was the first social encounter that I had with a girl in the last six months. Meeting her was really nice, and I hated to leave. It was like having a beautiful dream and then you wake up and wish you could go back. After leaving the club that night I headed to my job, and I cried for the first time in years.

By spring that year, I had saved enough money to try another round of applying to a foreign medical school. First, I arranged an interview with the Mexican embassy near 5ᵗʰ Avenue in New York City in order to apply to medical school in Guadalajara, Mexico. After a few weeks, I received an application and was so excited to have made it that far. I thought nothing could stop me now! It was April of 1976 when I was notified that a date for an interview was scheduled in Guadalajara, Mexico. The only images that I had of Mexico were from the cartoons that I saw as a kid. I pictured Mexicans riding donkeys, wearing sombreros, and living in adobes surrounded by cacti. I thought they were mostly farmers and laborers with little education. I figured Americans would be housed in modern trailers with the amenities of home but located in an arid desert with goats and cacti.

I was excited to go to Mexico for the medical school interview because now it seemed a reality—not just a dream. I headed to the airport by taking a bus from my house in New Jersey to the Port Authority in New York City. Then I had to take another bus to Kennedy Airport, where I boarded the plane and flew to Guadalajara, Mexico. I didn't know anything about Mexico or the city of Guadalajara—I only knew that when I got there, I had to find the medical school for my interview. When I finally arrived in Guadalajara, I got a taxi and headed for a hotel. As we drove through the city, I was shocked when I realized how culturally deprived I was. Guadalajara was magnificent and listed as one of the most beautiful cities in the world—and for good reason. There were beautiful trees and flowers in every yard as well as along the streets throughout the city. The homes were enclosed within whitewashed walls, affording the occupants security as well as privacy. The climate was perfect, sunny most of the year, warm but never humid, and if it rained, it was only at night during the rainy season.

The next day, I took a taxi to the medical school where I had my interview, which was conducted in English. The interview went well, leaving me feeling optimistic. I returned home and patiently waited to hear if I was accepted. After several weeks the letter from the school arrived stating that I was accepted. The next step was to contact other students in my area who were accepted to the same school and to see about our driving down to Mexico together. Luckily, I found a student, who lived close by that had a brother already studying medicine in Guadalajara. We made arrangements to drive down together in his small car. I packed a sleeping bag, five T-shirts, two pairs of pants, underwear, socks, and medical books. The trip took about three days to get to the Mexican border and another day to get to Guadalajara. There was no GPS system or cell phones, so we relied on maps to navigate over mountains and through villages and towns.

Eventually, in the early morning hours, we reached the Barrancas, the mountains near Guadalajara. It was still dark, and all we could see were thousands of twinkling lights from the city down below. My friend said, "Look at all those lights! All we need to do is find one of them—my brother's house."

Slowly, we drove down dark dangerous winding roads, overlooking steep drops with warning signs, "PELIGRO" (which means *danger* in Spanish). It was daylight when we finally reached the city, and then we had to navigate through the Spanish-named streets.

Eventually, we found his brother's house, and after a brief rest, they drove me downtown and dropped me off. I found a cheap hotel but needed to look for a permanent residence. I was told to go to a bookstore, called Sandy's, where American students hung out and posted rooms for rent and books for sale. There, I found an advertisement for a room available in a four-bedroom house shared by three other American medical students. For each student the rent was $100.00 a month, and the maid cost twenty dollars a week. I checked out the house and thought it was decent as well as being located in a quiet section of the city. I took the room and only had to buy a desk and chair because the bed was already there.

Although I was excited that I was going to start medical school in three months, I couldn't forget that all the classes, books, and tests were in Spanish. During the next three months, I settled into the daily routine of going to Spanish classes and learning about the city and culture. I shared the house with three other med students, some of whom had already been there from the previous semester. I had a limited budget, so my breakfast consisted of tortillas and eggs, lunch was peanut butter and jelly sandwiches, and dinner was quesadillas, lettuce, and carrots. The lettuce and carrots had to be soaked in iodinated water to kill the parasites. This monotonous menu continued for the entire time that I was there.

Learning Spanish in only three months before starting medical school seemed impossible. But, if others who went before me did it, then so could I. As I always said, *I can't be beat until I'm down and out and can't get up.* Three months later, on the first day of school, everybody panicked, not sure if we understood the instructions in Spanish. Because of the language barrier, the entire first semester was overwhelming. Books, lectures, and tests were all in Spanish. I studied as much as possible, starting before school, during school, and again after school until late at night. I needed to study the medical books, both in Spanish and English, which was tedious and frustrating. Needless to say, it was a constant struggle to learn the immense volume of information required in medical school, especially in another language.

My Spartan lifestyle, day in and day out, consisted of a monotonous diet of the same food, some exercise, and constant studying in both English and Spanish. At least we didn't have the burden of housekeeping which allowed more time for study. The maid washed clothes the old-fashioned way—on a washboard. She eventually wore out the knees on my only two pairs of pants. They needed to be patched, and I looked just like the kids in the old-time movies.

The only furniture that came with my room was the bed, which I soon discovered had bedbugs. They woke me up at night with painful bites, and when I reached down to feel where it hurt, I pulled off the blood-filled bugs. Naturally, I had to throw out the bed, mattress, and frame. I didn't have enough money to buy another bed, so I took the closest door off the hinges, laid it on cement blocks, and slept on it. Even without a mattress, it was better than lying on the cold tile floor.

The first semester was overwhelming—first the culture shock, then the volumes of material to be learned, and finally, the most stressful, studying in another language. Yet, there was one more kick in the groin—the discovery of a disability that plagued me all my life. I learned about it while reading my neurology textbook. I came across a neurological disorder called narcolepsy, defined as "the insatiable desire to sleep at inappropriate times." When I read that, my eyes welled up with tears, because all my life I thought that I was lazy, wanting to sleep on and off all day long. It was difficult staying awake while sitting, watching TV, or in a classroom listening to the teacher. Driving had been another nightmare, fighting the desire to sleep, while drinking coffee continuously in order to stay awake. Throughout high school I was unable to pay attention because I was constantly struggling to stay awake. I always thought that I could never amount to anything because I was lazy. Looking back, I realized that my poor performance in high school wasn't because I was stupid, but because I couldn't stay awake long enough to learn. Before I knew that I had narcolepsy, I thought that my sleepiness was partly due to boredom. Now, knowing that I had a real disability made me uncertain as to how I was going to handle learning the massive volume of material in medical school?

When medical school started, I was excited and nervous enough to stay awake in class for the first few days. But soon, I was back to struggling to stay awake, trying to pay attention during lectures, while fighting off sleep. I couldn't stay awake more than fifteen or twenty minutes, no matter how hard I tried. I was devastated and started to have doubts about getting through medical school. I read that there were medications for narcolepsy and hoped that they would help me. I went to a neurologist to see what medication might help and was prescribed dextroamphetamine, a very strong stimulant. I tried it for a week, but the side effects bothered me. Next, I tried Ritalin, another stimulant, and took it for a few weeks, but again, I couldn't tolerate it and stopped it abruptly. That led to a severe withdrawal, causing me to go into a deep depression. I never experienced anything like that and was so miserable that I wanted to quit medical school. Now, like so many times before, I felt hopeless that I could ever become a doctor. Not only did I have the problem of falling asleep in class, but also intolerance to the only medications that could help me. It seemed like a cruel trick to think that I came this far, overcoming the failures and humiliation during the last six years, and now I wanted to give up. I was so disgusted that I decided to quit school and walked out of class. I had to walk several miles to get back to my house. When my good friend David found out, he begged me not to quit. He said that there might be something else that could help me. He insisted on driving me to see a neurosurgeon who might be able to help. Unfortunately, the neurosurgeon couldn't help either, so now it was up to me to figure it out. This was it—now or never!

I knew that when I attended the lectures, I would never stay awake for more than fifteen minutes and would miss the rest of it. So, during the lectures I decided to try and read the subject matter until I fell asleep, wake up 15 or 20 minutes later, and continue reading where I left off. I repeated this routine in each class, and never listened to a lecture the entire time that I was in medical school. Of course, I never heard any announcements regarding schedules or test dates, so I relied on my friends to lead me around like a blind man. In spite of my inability to overcome narcolepsy and the language barrier, I managed to get a grade of B+ for the first semester. It was unbelievable…now after all those years, and all the setbacks, I was on my way to becoming a doctor.

After the first semester we were given a break for Christmas, which would be the first time in eight months that I was able to return home. I felt like a celebrity, anxious to return home, expecting my family and friends to share my excitement. I took a flight from Mexico to Texas, then had to take a connecting flight to New York. As I was getting off the plane in Texas, I waited in line behind a mother with a screaming baby. There were about 20 passengers in front of her and about another 30 passengers jammed behind me. While we were waiting to move forward, I tried to calm the baby that was facing me over the mother's shoulder. I did the "coochie, coochie, coo" routine; then suddenly the baby began to vomit. I tried to back up, but the passengers kept pushing forward, leaving me no room to avoid the shower of putrid sour milk. I was pissed off, and although I felt like choking the little bastard, I kept my cool. As soon as I got off the plane I immediately went to the men's room at the airport, stripped naked, and tried to wash up. I didn't have a change of clothes because my suitcase was in the baggage area, so I bought a tee shirt, and a fellow student gave me some cologne to mask the smell. I had another four-and-a-half-hour flight home. Finally arriving at Kennedy airport in New York, I was beaming with pride and feeling dignified as I got off the plane. I was expecting my family to be waiting, but I didn't know who was coming to pick me up, so I looked around for a familiar face.

Meanwhile, the other medical students met up with family members waiting to greet them. Gradually the other students and their families left while I waited, sitting on my suitcase. Finally, after about two hours, my sister and her friend showed up. She said that the reason she was late was because originally my brother was supposed to pick me up, but when he found out that the flight was delayed, he didn't want to wait. I wasn't upset about the wait because I was still excited, anticipating my parents' reaction when I got home. I couldn't hide how proud I was and how honored I felt to have become a member of the elite medical profession.

When I arrived home my parents' reaction wasn't at all what I had expected. Instead of being excited, they were skeptical and doubted that I would even go back to Mexico for the next semester. I felt hurt but understood their attitude considering that I had dropped in and out of five different colleges and already wasted money on another foreign medical school. I became accustomed to family and friends doubting that I would become a doctor. I ignored them, like I ignored my friends who years ago told me how some tough guy could kick my ass.

Beside my parents, another skeptic was my uncle Mike. He said in a patronizing tone, "I'll give you credit because you must have studied hard, and I doubt that you have the same smarts as your classmates." Condescendingly, he said that if I ever made it through the third year of school, he would pay for the fourth.

After Christmas vacation I returned to Mexico with $60.00 extra spending money, a gift from family members. This should have lasted until June, but the day that I returned, one of my fillings fell out. I went to a dentist, and he charged me exactly $60.00 to fill it. What else was new?

During the second semester I became more comfortable living in Mexico, and that was when I started my business of selling used books. I bought a bicycle and peddled around Guadalajara carrying a backpack filled with used books. I bought the books from graduating students and sold them to first semester medical students. That supplemented my income for the next three years. Another source of income was a student loan of a thousand dollars, interest-free, from a Jewish fraternity based in New York. So, even though I was Catholic, I joined the Jewish fraternity and became its president.

One of the medical school courses was otolaryngology, the study of ear, nose, and throat diseases. It required cadaver skulls to demonstrate the exam of ear canals. The residents who taught the course threatened to fail us if we didn't bring in human skulls with the ear canals intact. We heard of a cemetery that sold decomposed bodies for fifteen dollars. We went to the cemetery and found a man that agreed to sell us a body. He dug it up while we waited, then gave it to us in an empty cement bag. We took it home and noticed that pieces of nylon socks were still attached to the foot bones. Apparently, nylon doesn't deteriorate quickly. And patches of scalp with hair on it were still attached to the skull. To remove the scalp, we had to boil the skull in a pot on the kitchen stove and then scrape it off. Next, we took a hacksaw and sawed the skull in half, front to back, so that we would have two ear canals to give the teachers.

To learn anatomy, we had to dissect cadavers which were first preserved in vats of formaldehyde, which caused the skin to have a dark gruesome appearance. In order to retrieve the bodies before dissection, they had to be raised out of the large vats by a motorized winch. Meat hooks were placed in both ear canals, then the cadavers were slowly lifted out of the formaldehyde, head first. Next it was followed by the torso, then the rest of the body. It looked like a horror movie, with the body raised up out of the vat and the formaldehyde dripping down. Sometimes we would get an entire body to dissect, but mostly just an arm or a leg.

In 1978, my first summer vacation from medical school, I decided to get a ride with a classmate to his home in California, then hitchhike from there back to New Jersey. After driving through Mexico, we finally were about to cross the border, when suddenly a Mexican border patrol car sped up beside our van with machine guns pointed at us. As soon as I stopped driving, the border patrol agent jumped out and said that I was supposed to have stopped when the other border agent waved his hand. I said that I saw him wave his hand up and down and thought he meant for me to slow down.

He reprimanded me and then said we could go. Next, we crossed the border at San Diego and drove to Los Angeles where my friend's mother lived. She let me sleep there overnight; then the next day my friend drove me to Bakersfield and dropped me off to begin my cross country journey. I remember getting rides all through California, but I'll mention the things that stand out the most. The most prominent was in Northern California when I was freezing while trying to sleep in my skimpy sleeping bag. I never realized that it could be so cold in the summer. I couldn't sleep, so I walked to a truck stop and sat at the restaurant all night drinking coffee. The next day, I continued hitchhiking and finally arrived in San Francisco where I planned on meeting a Swedish girl that I dated three years prior. I called her, and she came and picked me up and took me to the house where she was working as an Au Pair. I stayed overnight at her house, but she had to leave early the next morning, so she dropped me off downtown San Francisco. From there I hitched a ride over the San Francisco Bridge and was invited to have a cup of tea on a houseboat by the guy who picked me up. I continued on up the California coast to Oregon and Washington State. Somewhere along the way, I was invited to stay overnight and use the shower at some guy's house. Later along the way I was picked up by a truck driver who let me sleep up in the bunk in his truck while he was driving. I was on the road for about a week when I finally reached Nebraska but couldn't go any longer because I was burning up as I hitchhiked on Route 80. The sun and wind were so intense that I tried to use an umbrella while I was standing on the side of the road, but the trucks whizzing by caused the umbrella to collapse inside out or blow out of my hand. That's when I decided to call it quits and backtracked to the nearest airport and flew back to New Jersey.

During the second year I started to date my teacher, a doctor doing her social service. Her name was Alma, and she helped me learn Spanish much more easily. I could ask her a question in English and ask her how to say it in Spanish. Two years later, at age thirty, I married Alma, who was five years younger than me. I was expecting her to start a residency after I graduated medical school and returned to the United States.

Each day of the next two years spent studying medicine in Mexico brought me closer to reaching my goal. I lived only to learn medicine and managed to get by on basic necessities. Every day I ate the same monotonous diet, tortillas and eggs for breakfast, peanut butter and jelly sandwiches for lunch, and for supper, quesadillas, carrots, and lettuce. After the exhausting studying in two languages and the multiple weekly exams, I finally graduated in 1981 at the age of thirty-one. All along, what seemed impossible slowly became believable, knowing that now I could look back and say, *I made it!*

After graduation, I had two months off before starting an internship called the Fifth Pathway at Hackensack Hospital, in Hackensack, New Jersey. Anyone who graduated from a Mexican medical school was required to do that internship in order to be equal to an American medical school graduate. Not only was this an extra year without pay, but it cost $2,500 to enroll in the program.

When I found out about the cost I wanted to cry, because I didn't have the money and it would be one more year before I could get paid as a resident.

I was broke, so my wife and I had to move into my parents' house, where we set up a bedroom in the attic. There was barely enough room for a double bed, which was positioned under a sloping roof, preventing you from sitting up if you were on the side next to the wall. On the opposite side, I had a narrow recliner squeezed in next to the head of the bed. There was only a small radiator that was barely able to give out enough heat to keep us warm, so it was always cold in the winter making it necessary to go downstairs to get dressed. We only had fans to keep us cool in the summer, but they were never enough to make us comfortable.

The two months that I had off before starting in Hackensack Hospital, I had to earn some money, so I took a job landscaping, earning four dollars an hour, working from 7 a.m. until 1 p.m. Finally, in August, I started the internship at Hackensack Hospital. This was it; I was a real doctor with a white coat and stethoscope hanging on my neck. The first day I had to attend the routine orientation for new interns. It was the second day—a day that I'll never forget. After making rounds, I thought that I had finished charting, and I had walked away from the nurse's station, when suddenly the nurse called out, "DOCTOR, you need to sign the lab request."

Time stood still, as I turned around and realized that moment in time was etched in stone. This was the first time someone called me *DOCTOR*!

Even though we were officially doctors, residents in the fifth pathway were not allowed to order medications. During my rotation in the emergency department, the paramedics asked me if I wanted to go on a cardiac arrest call. I agreed because I had only seen a cardiac arrest in the hospital, not out in the field. When we arrived CPR had already been started, so the paramedics attached the monitor which showed asystole—no heartbeat. Immediately, one paramedic intubated the patient to provide oxygen while the other inserted an IV to administer medications. The paramedics were unaware of my Fifth Pathway status, which prohibited me from giving orders, so they asked me if they could start the medications while we watched the monitor. I had seen the routine many times, the chest compressions, the oxygen administered, and the meds given, but I never gave orders.

Here I was, wearing my white lab coat, my stethoscope hanging on my neck, and my eyes fixated on the rhythm displayed on the monitor. The paramedics assumed that I was allowed to give orders so they asked me if they could give the routine meds per protocol. What was I supposed to say, "I can't give orders because I'm not a real doctor"? Not only was I not allowed to give orders, but I had never run a code before. So, I agreed to each one of the meds that they requested, knowing that it was the same routine that they had followed many times. After about 10 minutes on scene, the hospital base station medical command contacted the paramedic for an update on the patient's status. The paramedic answered the call and said that Dr. Castellano was on scene giving orders.

"What!?" shouted the base station emergency doctor, "He can't give orders!" The paramedics looked at me confused, wondering why I didn't tell them that I couldn't give orders. When we returned to the hospital, the doctor in charge of medical command reamed out the paramedics and said that they had to erase the recorded transcription.

All through medical school I had wanted to become a family doctor, but that changed during my Fifth Pathway internship at Hackensack Hospital. It was after the chief surgical resident gave us a lecture on the surgeon's "God-like image," I knew that was what I wanted. I decided to look for surgical residencies in rural areas in New England, New York State, and Pennsylvania. After going to different interviews, driving hundreds of miles throughout those states, I found one in Johnstown, Pennsylvania, that appealed to me.

I interviewed at Conemaugh Memorial Hospital in Johnstown, Pennsylvania, in the late fall, and I was accepted during the interview. I was flattered, because traditionally it wasn't until the following March that the residency programs decided which candidates would be accepted. I felt proud to think that I was chosen on the spot, ahead of all other applicants. When I returned to Hackensack Hospital after the interview, I bragged to my colleagues about my early acceptance into the surgical residency. Some looked skeptical, wondering why I was chosen before the "match" in March. I thought that I was chosen because of my merits and the favorable impression that I had made during the interview.

I was 32 years old when I finally finished the internship at Hackensack and moved to Johnstown to start my surgical residency. I didn't have any money to rent an apartment, so I borrowed the money from my mother, planning on paying her back in the next few months. Unfortunately, the secretary that arranged the paperwork for credentialing incoming doctors screwed up, and I was prohibited from working until the matter was resolved. I started to panic because I didn't have any money or a credit card, so if I didn't get paid, I couldn't buy food or gas. Fortunately, I was still paid until the paperwork was completed which was about a month later.

Shortly after I started the residency, I found out that the program was on probation and would close at the end of the year unless they could prove to the board that they met the required benchmarks. That's when I realized why I was accepted at my interview months before the match: they had few potential candidates interested in a program on probation. They needed residents to do slave labor so that the attending doctors would have less paperwork and phone calls, and in return, they were supposed to teach the residents hands-on surgical techniques. That rarely happened because Conemaugh Memorial Hospital was a community hospital with a strong middle-class population who had health insurance. The patients would say, "I don't want a resident operating on me."

The entire first year was overwhelming because of the 36-hour shifts and the 100-plus hour work weeks. Luckily, I found a way to overcome my phobia in math when I calculated drug doses using decimals. I saw .01 as 1 cent, .1 as 10 cents, etc., so a 70 kg patient whose dose of a medication was

.02 mg /kg would need 70 x .02 mg, which is 70 x 2 cents = $140 or 140 mg. Besides the grueling schedule required during a surgical residency, my narcolepsy was a constant curse, sapping my energy from comfortably performing the daily routines. Intermittently throughout the day I attempted to escape to the on-call room to take a 5-minute nap. It was painful to try and go without any naps, making me so irritable that sometimes I wondered how I would be able to endure the next years. However, as tough as it was struggling with narcolepsy, I never compromised patient care.

In addition, I had to sweat it out not knowing if our program would be cancelled by the end of the year. If so, we would have to scramble all over again looking for another first-year spot. I felt like I was a medical student again, holding retractors for the surgeon, making rounds on patients, and dictating discharge summaries. We were treated like slaves, degraded, and unappreciated.

Later in the year I discovered that my surgical residency was one of the last community surgical programs in the country, because the American Board of Surgery realized that the hands-on training was weak due the aforementioned middle-class population's attitude. The best programs were in the inner-city hospitals, where the indigent population had little choice about who operated on them. I was on pins and needles throughout that entire first year, not knowing if my residency would be approved by the American Board of Surgery. Finally, at the end of the year we were given three more years of probation. I was still fearful, because if we didn't get approval after the fourth year, I would be left hanging to find a surgical residency in order to complete the fifth year.

By the end of the first year, I had held retractors for the surgeons most of the time and had done very little surgery myself. I hoped that in the next four years I would have more hands-on surgical training, enabling me to develop the skills to operate on my own.

At the end of that first year, I was allowed one week of vacation. My wife and I had bought non-refundable discounted round-trip tickets from Pittsburgh to Acapulco, Mexico, which was her hometown. She hadn't been home for over a year and was anxious to see her family. The flight left at 9 a.m. from Philadelphia, so we had to leave in the early morning hours from Johnstown, which was about 4-1/2 hours away. While we were driving in my old Toyota on the Pennsylvania Turnpike, I suddenly heard a loud bang, and the car stopped. I didn't know what happened, but I knew that it was serious. It was in Harrisburg, which was still about two hours away from Philadelphia. There was a state police barracks on the other side of the turnpike, so I jumped over the guard rails and went over to the barracks to find out if any kind of transportation was available. The State Trooper there said that he heard the bang from his headquarters and that my motor was destroyed. He said that the car would be towed to a junkyard and that I would have to come back and turn the title over in order to sell it. Then he said that there was no bus service to Philadelphia, but he would call a trooper to take us to the next rest stop. When the trooper arrived, we put our luggage in the trunk, and a few miles down the road, we were dropped off at the closest rest stop. I didn't know how we could ever make it to the airport on time. I stood with my wife on the shoulder of the road with our luggage and tried to hitchhike. My wife started crying, knowing that she would never get home to see her family. It was still dark, and the chance of getting a ride was nearly impossible. I decided to try and get a ride from a person stopping to get gas at the service station. When a car finally stopped to get gas, I approached the driver who was a woman. I told her that I was with my wife, and I explained our situation of trying to get to Philadelphia, and I offered to pay for her gas. She agreed but said that she could only take us as far as a bus stop on the outskirts of Philadelphia. I was on pins and needles during the two-hour drive, doubtful that we would arrive on time. Finally, we arrived at the bus stop close to 9 a.m., the time the plane was scheduled to leave. Although desperate, we still had hope that the plane might be delayed, so we boarded the bus and headed towards the airport. The anxiety produced by the snail's pace through morning traffic, frequent red lights, and the interrupted stops, made me want to scream. It was already past 9 a.m. while we were still on the bus, with little hope of ever getting on the plane. The tickets were non-refundable, and my vacation time slot was inflexible, so if we missed this trip, we would have to wait a year for another opportunity. Around 9:30 a.m. we arrived at the airport convinced that it was too late, but we still decided to check in. Miraculously, the plane was delayed and we were able to get on the flight, and made it to see my wife's family. Still, I had to face the fact that we only had $150 which we had to save until we came back from vacation. We couldn't spend any money in Acapulco, so we stayed at my wife's family's house the entire week.

We returned to Philadelphia after a week in Acapulco and had to find a way to get back to Johnstown, 4-1/2 hours away. It was after midnight, and we had to take a taxi from the airport to the bus station in downtown Philadelphia. We had to wait more than an hour for the next bus in an area that was dangerous, inhabited by drunks, the homeless, and people strung out on drugs. I was apprehensive and hyper-vigilant, carefully sizing up every individual as a potential threat. I didn't see any police, which added to my stress.

Finally, we boarded the bus and eventually made it to Breezewood where I made a phone call to our neighbor asking her to come and get us even though it was about 3:30 a.m. By the time we arrived home in Johnstown it was almost 7 a.m., and I was scheduled to work that day. I called one of my surgical colleagues, who gave me a ride to work. I had no car and only $75.00 to my name. I didn't want to ride a bike to work, so I asked my parents for a loan so that I could buy a used car. My mother asked why I wouldn't buy a new car, then make payments over the next three years. She offered to loan me $1,000 to put down, and then I would make monthly payments. I was

33 years old and never thought of buying anything without paying cash. I never bought anything on credit, nor had a credit card, so this was a convenient way to make life more comfortable. Following my mother's advice, I bought a new Chrysler K car, the budget-friendly car that Lee Iaccoca came up with which enabled Chrysler to bail out of bankruptcy. The car only cost $7,000.00 and was equipped with bench seats, a stick shift, and a cassette player. During the first year we had lived paycheck to paycheck, barely able

to meet our expenses. We almost never went out to eat, and only allowed ourselves an occasional treat, a slice of pie each.

I was 33 years old when I started my second year of surgical residency. Nothing changed much during that year; holding retractors and doing scut work was a daily grind. One of the senior surgical residents earned some extra money doing pre-op physicals for the surgeons that were not affiliated with the program. The resident had to go away one weekend, so he asked me if I wanted to earn $20 doing a physical. I jumped on the opportunity, and for the first time I had enough money to take my wife out to eat.

It was 1984, during my third year, when things became more exciting. I was sent to Baltimore to do a three-month rotation in the world-famous Shock Trauma Center. There I saw everything that a trauma surgeon would handle. There were victims of gang violence with multiple gunshot wounds and complicated trauma patients sent from other hospitals. My first day I was told to run to the helicopter pad on the roof of the hospital to receive a trauma victim. I didn't know how to get there, so I was told to follow the trail of blood to the elevator and go to the roof. When I got there, the trauma nurses were already waiting. Minutes later the helicopter arrived, and we all ran to it, hunched over to avoid the rotating blades. The patient was put on the gurney and rushed down the elevator to the emergency department where a team of doctors was waiting. There the patient could go directly to the adjacent operating room if necessary.

During the three months at Shock Trauma, I saw injuries that I would have never seen in my rural residency program. Besides trauma, I spent a month in the neurosurgical ICU, managing head and spinal cord injuries. The residents didn't have a call-room, so we found an unused part of the old hospital building to take naps. The room smelled musty from the sweat of five or six exhausted residents jammed into one room, resting on bunk beds with bare mattresses. I didn't care because we were on call for 36 hours, and any chance to take a cat nap was a luxury.

One of the young trauma surgeons was Dr. Ganz, who was revered because he was on the trauma team at the Georgetown University Hospital in Washington, D.C., when President Reagan was shot. He helped operate on the president and told us that just before President Reagan was put under anesthesia, he said to the operating team, "I hope you're all Republicans."

Dr. Ganz was a great teacher and only a few years older than me. One day we were in a conference room waiting for the speaker, and Dr. Ganz sat next to me. Our conversation revolved around the construction of the new hospital, and I casually mentioned my experience as a union carpenter working on the construction of the New Jersey College of Medicine and Dentistry in Newark. He was shocked and looked at me in disbelief, wondering how I could go from carpentry to medical school, and now a surgical resident. He said that he never heard of anybody making such a radical transition and was impressed by my story. I didn't think of it as anything special because, although there were many disappointments and roadblocks along the way, I never lost sight of what I could be.

While I was at Shock Trauma, President Reagan was scheduled to give a speech in Baltimore, so a private trauma area was reserved for him. We were unaware that our trauma team had background-checks by the secret service, because my team was on duty during the President's visit to Baltimore.

I saw numerous victims of gunshot wounds from gang violence, but some stand out among the rest. One, in particular, was transferred from another hospital after receiving multiple blood transfusions for a bullet wound to his abdomen because no surgeon had been available to operate on him. Upon arrival, we immediately took him to the operating room and opened his abdomen. The amount of blood that flowed out looked like a bathtub overflowing, covering the floor with a puddle of blood. This was the accumulation of the man's entire blood volume plus the multiple transfusions trapped in his belly.

Another dramatic case was an elderly grandmother stabbed multiple times in the chest by a 13-year-old boy. The woman had been babysitting for her grandchildren when she heard a knock on her door. When she opened the door, the boy rushed in and stabbed her for no reason. Upon arrival she was awake and talking but started to deteriorate rapidly. She developed cardiac tamponade, an accumulation of blood in the sac around her heart which constricted the pump function. We rushed her to the operating room and performed a cardiac window. This procedure consisted of a scalpel incision in the area by the solar plexus, creating an opening in the sack around the heart, and then inserting a drain so that blood could be evacuated. She survived the operation but died shortly after. That night on the news from the local TV station, the story of the crime was revealed, and the boy was arrested.

Saving a life by opening a chest in the emergency room is the most rewarding dramatic surgical procedure that most doctors will never have a chance to see. The case that I'm referring to was of a 40-year-old man who was stabbed in the heart and went into cardiac arrest in the emergency department. We couldn't wait to go to the operating room, so we immediately opened his chest in the emergency department. We exposed his heart and noted the puncture wound that caused his arrest.

We immediately started massaging his heart, equivalent to chest compressions, while we sutured the hole shut using felt pledgets to anchor the sutures. Once the wound was closed, we shocked the heart out of ventricular fibrillation to a normal sinus rhythm and restored the normal pump function. The patient's heartbeat was now strong and his blood pressure normal. The next day when I checked in on him, he was wide awake and doing well. I examined him and noted that his bandage was dry, and his vital signs remained stable. When I asked him if he remembered what happened, he shocked me and said that he was in another place, a place that he couldn't describe—a place that he had never been before. I didn't tell him that the night before, he died in the emergency department right before our eyes.

One of the trauma fellows, named Dr. Matt Indek, was doing the extra year after graduating from a surgical residency in order to become a trauma surgeon. He was the leader of our trauma team, and we were training under him. One day we were talking about how the American Board of Surgery strictly prohibited surgical residents from moonlighting because they felt that it would limit the resident's time off needed to study. I had secretly moonlighted in different emergency departments during my residency because I needed the money. I didn't think that any other surgical residents moonlighted, because of the Surgery Board's restrictions, but I remembered being surprised seeing an article on the front cover of a *Parade* Magazine. The cover showed the picture of a surgery resident from Charity Hospital in Louisiana who described the grueling hours he worked plus the extra time he spent moonlighting. When I mentioned that the surgical resident on that cover was the only other surgical resident besides myself that moonlighted, Dr. Indek said that it was him on the cover. I couldn't believe the coincidence of actually meeting the doctor whose picture I had seen on the cover of a national publication.

After 3 months at Shock Trauma, I returned to my surgical program in Johnstown, Pennsylvania. It was my third year, and I was doing the same routine—holding retractors, rounding on patients, and doing discharge summaries. Later that year, I was assigned a two-month rotation on the cardiothoracic service at Temple University Hospital in Philadelphia. My job was to manage patients needing bypass surgery or heart transplants, neither of which I had any experience with. I was sent from my program in Johnstown and told that I would have to find my own place to live for the two-month rotation. I wasn't familiar with Philadelphia, so I had to drive around looking for a decent place to live. I carried my .38 revolver, not knowing where I would wind up, and especially because I had my wife with me. She was about two months pregnant and suffering from hyperemesis gravidarum while we searched for an apartment. We found one in Manayunk which seemed like a nice location, but it was sparsely furnished. It had a bed and TV and that was all. Over the next week she became dehydrated from vomiting, so I took her to the Abington Hospital where she was admitted overnight for fluid replacement. After being discharged, she decided it would be best to go back and stay with her family in Mexico while I spent the next two months in Philadelphia.

At Temple, the head of cardiothoracic surgery was Dr. Jack Kolph, the son of the world-famous Dr. Jacob Kolph who invented the renal dialysis machine. It was an interesting story how Dr. Jacob Kolph experimented with juice cans, foil, and wires to make the machine, while working secretly under the Nazi occupation of Holland during World War II. After the war the Dutch family immigrated to the United States when Dr. Jack Kolph was just a teenager.

The first month was very stressful on my cardiothoracic rotation at Temple because I was on my own, making rounds without any senior resident. Even worse, there weren't any teams to start IV's, no lab techs to draw blood, and no respiratory therapists to get blood gases. When I started to manage critical patients in the cardiothoracic unit, I was shocked when a nurse refused to draw blood from a patient and take it down to the lab. Another time, the nurses refused to take the sample of blood gases to the lab from a patient that I had intubated and that needed me to manage their heart rate and blood pressure. They would say, "You get the blood!" and "Take it down yourself!"

I wasn't used to these inner-city, tough, assertive nurses. I had always worked in an environment where, whatever the doctor needed, the nurses would comply. Their refusal to help me was interfering with my managing critical pre- and post-op patients in the cardiothoracic unit.

Besides managing critical patients, I assisted Dr. Kolph and the other surgeon, Dr. Mike Deeb, on bypass surgery and heart transplant procedures. The heart transplant is still the most amazing thing that I have ever seen. Before the transplant, the donor organ has to be present, shipped in a cooler like one that holds a six-pack of beer. It's transported either by private vehicle or flown in from anywhere in the country. The recipient patient has to be put on bypass first, in preparation to receive the donor heart, then the non-beating donor's heart is positioned in the chest. Next, the blood vessels are carefully sutured in place, and when that's complete, the surgeon injects adrenaline into the donor's motionless heart. Seconds later there is a barely perceptible twitch visible, followed by several more twitches, then finally a contraction of the entire heart. It was an emotional experience to see a divine creation respond to a human intervention.

After the first stressful month on the cardiothoracic service, I was more comfortable starting the second month. I was almost living at the hospital, working 14-hour days, 7 days a week. I assisted on many cardiac bypass cases, sometimes helping harvest the veins from the legs. I learned a lot of critical care during the first month, and by the second month, I was managing patients on my own. I was flattered when Dr. Kolph said that he was confident that I could manage the cardiothoracic service on weekends without him.

Towards the end of my rotation, I was in the OR observing a third-year surgical resident doing a biopsy of the heart on a transplant patient, to check if there was any rejection. I had been caring for the patient in the cardiothoracic unit for the last week, after he had his transplant. The biopsy was routine on every post-op transplant patient, but it was this resident's first time doing the procedure. I watched as he carefully inserted a catheter into the jugular vein, then into the vena cava, and finally into the heart. He took a piece of tissue, trying to be careful not to perforate the heart wall. The procedure was uneventful, and afterward the patient returned to the cardiothoracic unit. About an hour later I was called STAT to that unit because the patient was having problems. I rushed to the unit and noticed that his breathing was labored and his color grey, a result of the biopsy accidentally perforating the heart. The blood leaked into the sack surrounding the heart causing a life-threatening condition called cardiac tamponade. It needed to be surgically resolved immediately by removing the blood-filled sack and then inserting a drain to prevent further accumulation. I notified the surgeon, and we rushed the patient to the OR and saved the patient's life. Over the next week, I saw the patient every day, and he was doing well.

There was another heart transplant patient in the unit who I got to know well over several weeks. He was recovering from his transplant without any problems. He was a Philadelphia businessman, and we talked often about our backgrounds. Of all the patients I saw, he was the one I enjoyed the most. On the last day of my rotation, I had one more surgical case scheduled in the morning, then afterward I hoped to finish my charts and leave. The patient scheduled was my friend, the Philadelphia businessman, and the procedure was to biopsy the heart muscle to rule out rejection. This was my last day, and I wanted to leave there with a good reputation. I was hoping that the surgeon would do the biopsy, but instead, he wanted me to do it, and the patient consented. I thought, *here I am, ready to leave, and now I have to do one of the most delicate procedures on a patient that I considered a friend.* What made it worse was my witnessing the resident perforating another patient's heart the week before.

I did the biopsy and hoped and prayed that it went well. Like the other patient, after the procedure was finished, he was stable and returned to the unit, but we had to wait a few hours to know for sure that there were no complications. After I left the operating room, I went to finish all my charts, when suddenly my pager went off. STAT 7th floor, the cardiothoracic ICU. My heart stopped— my patient—my friend...I perforated his heart. Without hesitating, I took the stairs instead of the elevator, and as I was running up the 7 flights, I thought that on my last *day, my reputation was ruined.*

Finally, out of breath, I reached the 7th floor and expected the worst. Instead, I was shocked— next to the nurses' station I saw all my cardiac patients, some in wheelchairs, and some standing, all in their hospital gowns and slippers. Among them was my friend, the patient that I had done the biopsy of his heart that morning. Those tough nurses, who initially gave me a hard time, were there too, smiling, and presented me with a cake. Even the other third-year resident, the one who had perforated a patient's heart the week before, was there smiling, knowing how surprised I was.

Finally, my patient, the one whose heart I biopsied that morning, was laughing, and said, "We knew that if you were called STAT to the 7th floor, you would have thought that you perforated my heart. We all knew that you would run up; that way we could surprise you and thank you."

Before I left the hospital that day, I had to stop by the office for my evaluation. Dr. Deeb told me that he and Dr. Kolph were more than satisfied with my work, and then he said, "You weren't the smartest resident to rotate through here, but you were definitely the hardest working and most dedicated."

After the Temple Hospital rotation, I returned to my residency program in Johnstown and was close to the end of my third year. My pregnant wife also returned from Mexico and was in her first trimester. I started back on my familiar routine, taking calls every fourth night making rounds on post-op surgical patients. One night I was paged to go to the ER to admit a patient. The nurse said that the patient was terminally ill from cancer and was to be admitted for comfort measures only. She said that the patient was in room 3, with the curtain closed to maintain privacy. When I went over and opened the curtain I was shocked at the sight of a bald emaciated skeletal figure, weighing no more than 50 pounds. The only way that I knew it was a woman, was by the lipstick, earrings and gold necklace. She was about middle-age and dying from advanced cancer. In spite of her condition, she didn't complain and knew that the end was near.

To see this dying woman still trying to look her best touched my heart. I couldn't hold back my emotions and told her how deeply I was touched, seeing how she maintained her dignity to the very end. I was so impressed with this remarkable person, I had to find out more about her. Later that night after she was admitted, I stopped by her room to check on her. I spent over an hour listening to the story about her life and how cancer cut short her plans to travel. She said when she was about 40, her mother was diagnosed with cancer and needed her help. She had never been married, so her mother was able to get her full attention over the next several years, postponing her dream to travel. Unfortunately, as soon as her mother died, she was diagnosed with cancer and never did have a chance to travel. During my visit I was interrupted when I was called to see a complicated post patient. I hated to leave and told her that I would check back with her on my rounds in the morning. The next morning, I went to her room and her bed was empty. I asked the nurse where the patient was...the one that I admitted the night before. She said that she died a few hours ago. I didn't know which was worse, the sadness that I felt from her dying or from my loss of ever knowing this remarkable person. In the short time that I spoke to her, I learned that one's dignity can be maintained, in spite of the worst of circumstances.

It was about a month later, while I was making rounds, that the charge nurse asked me if I had been on call Saturday night four weeks ago. Knowing that my call schedule was every other weekend, I said that I would have been on call that weekend. She told me that her terminally ill aunt was admitted that Saturday night and died the following morning. At the funeral home, family members mentioned to her that they came to visit her aunt in the middle of the night. Her dying aunt told the family how comfortable she felt after some young doctor came to her room and spent time talking to her. The nurse said that nobody knew who the doctor was, but she thought it might have been me.

I said, "Yes, it was."

✶✶✶

In order to make extra money, residents sometimes moonlighted working in Emergency Rooms. During my second year, I was eligible to moonlight, but I waited to become certified in ATLS, ACLS, and PALS. Those courses would enable me to stabilize patients in life-threatening situations. I finally started moonlighting in my third year because I had to first complete the PALS (pediatric life support) course before I would allow myself to work in the ER. One day an opportunity arose when another resident, who had signed up for a moonlighting shift, couldn't go. He asked me if I would do it, and I readily agreed. He explained that it was a night shift, 7 p.m. to 7 a.m., at a hospital about two hours away. The pay was $25 an hour, so I would earn $300 for the shift. I was 34 years old, and this was the first time I was able to make any money as a doctor. I was so excited, and I had the $300 already spent in my head before I even started the shift.

After about a 2-hour drive, I arrived at this rural hospital and went directly to the "Emergency Room" entrance. It was in the basement of the hospital and the entrance was through a screen door. It was July, and there was no air conditioning, so the screened windows were left open. This was the classic, old emergency room located in the basement of the hospital, with exposed pipes and electric wires visible on the ceiling.

Because it was "on the spur of the moment" that I was replacing the resident who was scheduled to work, I hadn't been credentialed yet in that hospital. When I arrived, no one knew me, and no one knew that I wasn't credentialed. No one questioned me because they were accustomed to different residents moonlighting at their hospital. I remember the nurses' names: one was Jim, the other Jackie; and neither one knew that it was my first time moonlighting. I was completely on my own, without any backup, and I didn't know any of the doctors working there. Because it was a rural area, the nearest hospital was about thirty miles away, so I was apprehensive about what could come through the door next. Thank God the shift was manageable and uneventful, and when it was over, I expected the relieving doctor to be there at 7 a.m. I was in a hurry to get back to my residency program, but I couldn't leave until he arrived. By 7:15, I asked the nurse when the doctor was coming in. She said that he usually didn't arrive until 7:30, and if there were a cardiac arrest, they would call a local doctor to come. I couldn't believe it, but I had to rush back to my residency program in time to start rounds. This was a rural hospital with a laid-back attitude, and the nursing staff and doctors seemed to function at a slower pace.

A month later, I found another hospital that needed a doctor to moonlight, and it was also about two hours away. I had to wake up and leave Johnstown around 5 a.m., then use a map to guide me through rural Pennsylvania. Eventually I arrived at the hospital, located in Du Bois, tired but excited about working in the ER. After doing one shift there I was asked to come back a few weeks later. It was only the third time that I moonlighted in an ER, but it turned out to be one of the most stressful situations that I would encounter over the next 33 years.

The shift started out with the routine sore throats and colds, when suddenly the doors flew open, and a mother rushed in holding her 6-month-old baby, screaming, "My baby can't breathe! She swallowed a tooth!" The baby was blue, not breathing, unresponsive, and barely had a pulse. I grabbed the baby girl from the mother, laid her down on the gurney and told the nurse to give her oxygen by face mask while I got ready to intubate her. While doing that, I couldn't ignore the mother's screaming, "Don't let my baby die!"

I was so nervous that my knees were shaking and must have looked like a dog's tail wagging.

When I opened the baby's mouth there was no foreign body, so I instantly proceeded to intubate her. As soon as I inserted the tube into her trachea and administered oxygen, she immediately pinked up and started to move. Before I could check the correct placement of the tube, she vomited the tooth up the tube and started screaming. Never before or since, has any music sounded as beautiful as that baby's scream. I was drained emotionally and physically after that. I had been so focused on saving the baby that I was unaware of how much time had passed. When the baby was okay, I was surprised to see that there were a half a dozen people there to help. I wasn't aware that the ER nurse had called a pediatric code as soon as the baby arrived. I wasn't sure how long I was working on the baby before she was free from the obstruction and breathing on her own. It seemed like an eternity, but when I asked the nurse how much time had passed before the baby was back to normal, she said, "About two minutes."

It turned out that the baby's mother, Brenda, was a nurse and worked for the local pediatrician, Dr. S. When I asked Brenda how the baby got ahold of a tooth, she said that her six-year-old boy had a loose tooth, and when he pulled it out, he put it on the counter next to the baby's highchair. The baby must have reached over and put it in her mouth and started choking and then stopped breathing.

The years passed, but I never forgot that day in the little hospital in Du Bois, Pennsylvania.

Getting back to my residency…I was thirty-five, entering my fourth year of the surgical residency, and my wife was expecting our first child. I was scheduled to start a six-month rotation at the Veterans Hospital in Altoona, Pennsylvania. Becoming a father was the most important event in my life. I would have more time to spend with my family because the rotation at the Veterans Hospital was a lot less demanding. After the experience moonlighting, I realized that I loved emergency medicine more than surgery and wished that I would have chosen an emergency medicine residency. I no longer wanted to become a surgeon at that point, but I had only a little more than a year left before I would graduate from the surgical residency. I had already completed almost five years of postgraduate training—a year of internship and four years of surgical residency—and to give

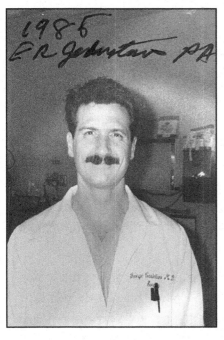

it up would make me ineligible to become a board-certified surgeon. If I quit, I wouldn't have any guarantee of future employment.

After I finished my six-month rotation at the VA, I returned to Johnstown to complete the remainder of my fourth year. My heart was no longer into surgery, and I couldn't work as hard as I had before. My attending surgeons noticed my lack of enthusiasm, so they asked the head of the department, Dr. Konvolinka, to have a talk with me. He said it was evident that I wasn't putting in as much effort as before, and he thought my priority now was being a father. He reassured me that I could finish out the next year and graduate if I wanted to, but he felt that I might regret it later because there were few jobs out there for general surgeons. He said that he didn't want to see me wind up an alcoholic in some remote town that had little need for a surgeon. Up until then, I was undecided about leaving surgery, but his advice convinced me. When he said that he felt that my heart was no longer set on becoming a surgeon, I was convinced that I would leave the surgical residency. I didn't realize, at that time, how difficult it was for him to tell me that it was better if I didn't finish the residency.

✶✶✶

I was nervous now that I wouldn't be a board-certified doctor, and although I could find jobs moonlighting, eventually board certification would be required. And now that I had a bigger responsibility being a father, without board certification there might not be any stable employment.

Now, at 36 years old, after years of overcoming numerous setbacks and humiliation, spending four years in a Mexican medical school, then slaving through a year of internship and four years of residency, I still had no future security. With a nine-month-old baby and a wife to support, I felt even more anxious and uncertain that I would find a hospital that would hire me without being certified. I must have been so depressed and didn't know it, because after talking to my uncle, he said that I needed to see a psychiatrist. I listened to him because he was so cynical and usually didn't trust doctors. So, I reluctantly arranged to have a psychiatric evaluation. I remember one of the tasks that the psychiatrist asked me to do was draw a clock. Till this day, I can't believe how I screwed up that simple task. I made the circle, but I couldn't arrange the spacing of the numbers. I spaced the numbers too close on one side and too far apart on the other. The psychiatrist must have realized that I was seriously depressed and said that he was concerned about me. The only solution to ease my apprehension about the future was to become board certified in another field of medicine. Family practice was the most logical alternative, but I would probably have to start as a first-year resident. It was depressing to think that I would have to start at the bottom in a residency, and work my way up, when I could have already been in my last year as a chief resident in surgery. I felt as if I were back as a beginner, the lowest of the low, when I should have been at the top, the highest of the high. I searched for the nearest family practice program that was accepting residents and found one in West Virginia. I eagerly applied and drove down to Morgantown, West Virginia, with my wife and nine-month-old daughter. The interview went well, and I was considered for a position that would allow me to start in a transition program between the first and second year. If all went well with the credentialing process, and I would start in July. It was somewhat comforting to know that at least I would be eligible to become board certified in another two-and-a-half years. With my anxiety put to rest, I signed up to start in the next 3 months and started looking for a house for sale. My wife and I found a house in Morgantown, close to the hospital, so I put down a deposit of $1,000 and applied for a mortgage. About a month later the program director called me and said that there was a problem with my credentials. He said that the state of West Virginia did not honor medical school graduates from Mexico who did the Fifth Pathway, so I couldn't be licensed to practice medicine in the state. Once again, I was screwed. Not only was I prohibited from getting a license in West Virginia, but I lost the $1,000 deposit that I put down on the house. The future was still uncertain, leaving me having to do moonlighting jobs in various emergency departments.

It was 1986, and there was a shortage of emergency medicine physicians, and more and more residency programs were starting up with the hope of graduating enough board-certified doctors to fill most emergency departments. I didn't want to do a three-year emergency residency program after already having completed a one-year internship and four years of surgical residency. In the meantime, even without board certification, I could probably find work for the next few years.

Eventually, I heard of an alternative route to become board certified in emergency medicine without doing a residency. It was by the practice route that would allow doctors to be grandfathered into the specialty. It was designed to help increase the number of board-certified emergency doctors, in addition to the residency programs. The requirements were to have completed 5,000 hours working in an emergency department over a 60-month period, and then to pass the same oral and written exam that was required of emergency medicine residents. Now I could look forward to working at something I loved—emergency medicine—and eventually become board certified.

I was 36 years old when I moved to Brookville, Pennsylvania, to start my first job in Brookville Hospital as a full-time emergency physician. I was scheduled to work 24-hour shifts and to do 15 shifts a month. I bragged that in one day I made $700, but it was a 24-hour day, not a normal 8-hour day.

Before I moved to Brookville, I heard that it was one of the most historically preserved towns in Pennsylvania, so I thought it would be sophisticated with a lot of culture. The reality was that "historically preserved" translated to "old," with almost no industry, and large numbers of workers unemployed, or at best, large numbers of workers at minimum-wage jobs. I couldn't believe it when I heard that the Brookville hospital was the largest employer in town. I should have done my homework before I decided that was where I wanted to live and raise a family. I was shocked when I found out that there were families there that had been on welfare for three generations. I never knew of able-bodied people who didn't work. Eventually, I worked in 11 different hospital emergency departments and discovered that every community had well-established second- and third-generation welfare families. Where I was raised in New Jersey, almost everybody worked. I never knew of any family members who didn't work. Even my father's friend Joe, who had excruciating back pain, still continued to work.

The three years that I worked in the Brookville Hospital was a gradual introduction to the multi-specialty emergencies for which an ER doctor was responsible. Unlike a big city hospital, the volume was less and the pace slower, but I still had to handle and stabilize life-threatening emergencies. Meanwhile, I had to continuously study in order to prepare for the boards. I was learning more and more, which increased my confidence considerably.

It was 1987, while living in Brookville, that my wife and I noticed that our 18-month-old daughter seemed to have lost weight and seemed to have become less active than she normally was. Something was not right, so I took her to the hospital to get a blood test. The lab tech, with 20 years' experience, was shocked when she drew the blood, and she said that she had never seen anything like it. She said that it looked like black water. Soon after that, the pathologist called me and said that he was confused and didn't know what to call it. He said that he couldn't find any evidence of cancer but thought it might be an overwhelming infection. He had another pathologist examine it, and she came to the same conclusion. The one thing that stood out was the low hemoglobin level of 5. The normal range was between 12 and 15. I had a very bad feeling that something was seriously wrong, such as leukemia, so I called Pittsburgh's Children's Hospital late that night and spoke to the on-call doctor. I told him the signs and symptoms, the lab results, and my worst fears. He said that I should bring her down as soon as possible. It was March 31, 1987, and snowing heavily, but I decided to go to Pittsburgh which was about a 1-hour-and-45-minute drive under normal conditions. We left at midnight and made it safely. At the hospital my daughter was initially examined by the resident, but we had to wait until the morning for the pediatrician to see her. I was scheduled to work a 24-hour shift that morning, so I called the ER director, Dr. Harvey, and asked if he could cover for me, explaining the serious condition my daughter was in. He emphatically said, "No!" So, I had to leave my wife and daughter, and drive back through a snowstorm, finally getting home about 4 a.m. I only got about two and a half hours of sleep before starting a 24-hour shift. It was April 1st, April Fools' Day—a day that I'll never forget. I called my wife several times to find out if the pediatrician had any answers. Finally, late in the afternoon, she called me, crying, and told me that the doctor said it was leukemia. Time Stood Still, and the word *Leukemia* was burned into my brain—like a hot branding iron searing a cow's hide. I remember exactly where I was standing in the nurses' lounge when I answered that call. The rest of the day was a blur, and I was numb and in shock. After the shift was over, I went home and collapsed, too weak to try and visit my wife and daughter who were both alone in Pittsburgh. I was so devastated and grief-stricken, that I did something I hadn't done since I was in grade school—I prayed!

I was sobbing and kissing pictures of Jesus, resorting to my childhood innocence. I was sick the next few days but kept calling my wife to see how my daughter was doing. Surprisingly, she responded to the chemotherapy well and was scheduled to be discharged at the end of the week.

During that first week after my daughter was diagnosed with leukemia, I felt as though I lost my manhood—neutered, without any thoughts of "intimacy."

The following week my daughter was to be discharged, so I went down to Pittsburgh to take her home, and upon seeing her, I was amazed at how good she looked. I was told that the prognosis was good which made me hopeful that she would do well. Suddenly, I felt like my old self, my manhood was restored, so I said to my wife, "I feel normal again."

She said, "I do too. I want to go shopping."

That wasn't the response that I was hoping for.

Thank God, my daughter did well, and the two years of the mild chemotherapy didn't have any negative effects. Ever since, I carry in my wallet the visitors pass that parents were given at Children's hospital. I think of it as the lucky winning ticket in a million-dollar lottery. My wife and I were optimistic that our daughter would eventually be cured, but one day while I was thumbing through the pages of a *Newsweek* magazine, the picture of a young girl's face caught my eye. The girl looked to be about five or six years old with dark hair and big brown eyes, a lot like my daughter. I can't describe why, but there was an eerie feeling about that picture. So, I quickly turned the pages. As I read on, I was haunted by that picture and had to go back and read why that girl's picture was there. My gut feeling was right because the advertisement was for the Make-A-Wish Foundation, and that girl was in remission from leukemia. I had never heard of the Make-A-Wish Foundation, which solicits donations to pay for the wishes of seriously or terminally ill children. I was really upset with this picture of the girl who looked healthy and a lot like my daughter. I was unnerved thinking that my daughter looked as good as this healthy-looking girl who was still considered terminal. So now my optimism was shattered because my daughter looked as healthy as that girl in the advertisement for the Make-A-Wish Foundation. I couldn't stand it, thinking that my daughter's healthy appearance during chemotherapy was just an illusion. So I called the Make-A-Wish Foundation and asked them about the picture of the girl in *Newsweek*. They said that she was diagnosed with leukemia at age three and now was about six years old. She was healthy and had been off chemotherapy for three years and was now considered cured. I blew up and asked why would you display a picture of a healthy girl in your advertisement for terminally ill kids? It makes me think that no matter how well they respond to chemo, and no matter how good they look, they are still going to eventually die. I told them that my daughter wasn't terminally ill, and they shouldn't put pictures of healthy kids in their advertisements. It makes parents like me think a healthy appearance is just temporary and that their kid is going to eventually relapse. They listened graciously to my complaint and then offered me a Make-A-Wish pass to any place that my daughter wanted. I emphatically said, "NO! Don't you get it? I won't accept the money to pay for a trip to Disney or some other childhood fantasy vacation because, by doing so, I'd be admitting that my child is terminally ill." I said, "Keep your money! I don't want it because my child is going to be cured."

1988

For Christmas of 1988, my wife's family came to visit us in Brookville and stayed about five days. Her mother and brother flew in from Mexico, and her other brother and her sisters came with their families. The night before Christmas Eve, I had planned to dress up as Santa Claus and entertain my friends' kids as well as my nieces and nephews. I had the costume ready and a tentative time scheduled for 7 p.m. Around 5 p.m., I decided to go to the local car dealership and check out a Lincoln and take it for a ride. When I returned the car, the boss invited me to the back of the showroom for his Christmas party. I declined the offer, but he insisted, and handed me a glass of whiskey. I really didn't want it, but I was hungry and started eating potato chips which made me very thirsty. The whiskey was convenient, so I started sipping it, and before I knew it, I was drunk. I lost all track of time. Suddenly, I was jolted back to reality when someone said my wife was on the phone and wanted to talk to me. I went to the other room to answer the phone, and it felt like I was walking on clouds. My wife started yelling at me because I sounded drunk, and she threatened to sue the car dealership if they tricked me into buying a car. The next thing that I remembered was being driven home and stumbling as I walked into the house. My wife's family watched as I tried to maintain my balance, holding onto the kitchen counter. The Santa Claus gig was definitely over, so my brothers-in-law decided to carry me upstairs and sober me up before I went to bed. They helped my wife undress me, then sat me on the toilet bowl. Next, they gave her a bag of ice to hold against my testicles while they both watched. I vaguely remember mumbling, "Ah, that feels good."

1989

After two years of chemotherapy, my daughter was considered cancer-free. The dark cloud lifted, so I decided to move to Du Bois, about 30 miles away. We bought an unsightly old ranch house, but it was located on three of the most beautiful lakefront lots. I intended to knock it down and build a beautiful new house, but when I approached my bank for a loan, they said that I had to pay off the remaining $70,000 mortgage. Now I was in a bind trying to figure out how long it would take to save up $70,000. I didn't want to wait years to save enough before I could build a new house, so I asked another bank if I could get a loan to build a house. When they said *okay*, I asked them if it mattered where I built it. They said that they didn't care, so I said that I was going to build it next to the old house, and I came up with an architectural plan incorporating the old house into the new one. That way, I could maintain the beautiful location on the lakefront property. I had an architect lay out the exterior design of the new and old houses joined together so that the builders would have an idea of the dimensions. I kept the old house almost undisturbed, except I had the roof raised to match the adjoining new house, and I had new windows installed. The interior remained structurally unchanged, but the rooms took on different purposes. What started out as an old ranch house blossomed into seven bedrooms, five bathrooms, and three fireplaces that were all brick in the front and on the sides. The back had a deck that was almost as long as the house and was protected by a roof. The entire front of the property was set off from the road by a magnificent, natural stone wall which opened to a winding driveway that went around the back to a basement garage. I was really proud, not only to have such a magnificent house, but to have had the imagination to incorporate the old house with the new. I received so many compliments about my house, and its location on the lake, that I felt that it was a landmark. Ever since I was a kid growing up in a blue-collar family, I wished that someday I wouldn't have to worry about money. I remembered how many times that I wanted what other people "had." Now, finally, I "had" what other people wanted.

Over the 17 years that I lived in Treasure Lake in Du Bois, we had jet skis, a speed boat, and canoes docked on our lake front property. It was more than I ever dreamed of, but it didn't feel like a home town. Treasure Lake was a private community with security guards at the entrance and a lot of the homes that were just vacation homes. On any given street there could be extravagant homes next to double wides. Many of the residents were transient, either middle management or health care professionals who stayed for a few years and then left. Numerous times we were saddened when several close friends were transferred after living there only 2 to 3 years. Many of the residents like us weren't from Du Bois, but moved to Treasure Lake because of the affordable housing and convenient location. The first few years we hardly knew anyone until our kids went to school. I decided to enroll my son and daughter in the Baptist Academy because I met some people who attended the Baptist Church. Although both my wife and I were Catholic we wanted to try a different church. We liked socializing after church service in the Baptist church and established a network of friends there. Our kids were enrolled in the Baptist Academy up until Ali was in fifth grade and Chris was in third grade, but we decided to switch back to the Catholic Church in order to enroll our kids in Catholic school. My daughter Ali and my son Chris grew up in Du Bois and graduated from Central Christian Catholic School. Ali played on a coed freshman and sophomore soccer team and was an avid reader. Chris was a skateboard fanatic, meanwhile teaching himself how to play the guitar and eventually established a band.

One day after school, Ali was talking to her classmate, and I overheard the classmate tell Ali about her friend who, as a baby, almost choked to death on a tooth. I was surprised, because I had never heard of another kid choking on a tooth. Then it struck me—it was here in Du Bois 12 years ago in a small rural hospital, that I saved a baby's life. I thought, *could it be possible that Ali's classmate's friend was the same girl who swallowed a tooth?* I couldn't remember the baby's mother's name, but I knew that she was a nurse who worked for a local pediatrician.

I asked Ali's friend if the girl's mother worked for Dr. S, and she said that she did. When she said the mother's name, it came back to me, and I asked my daughter if she knew the girl. She said yes and that the girl was a year ahead of her in the 7th grade. I couldn't believe it and had to call Dr. S's office to talk to the mother. When the nurse answered and said her name was Brenda, I told her who I was and that I was living in Du Bois and that my daughter went to the same school as her daughter. She said she couldn't believe it! We were both so emotional; I can't remember who was choked up more, the mother or me. A few weeks after that phone call, I volunteered to bring a cow's heart to my daughter's science class to show the anatomy and function of the heart. While I was at the school, I had the opportunity to meet the girl whose life I saved 12 years before. When I introduced myself, she started to cry and said, "I always wanted to meet you…the doctor who saved my life." I tried to hold back my emotions, but I know she saw how choked up I was.

While working full time as an emergency physician, I took on a job as a jail doctor, visiting the jail one day a week. Over the years, I saw some interesting cases. The most sensational one was when I had just started. A new warden was also hired at the same time. Within the first week a prisoner escaped, and the new warden felt responsible. The warden knew where the inmate lived and figured that the inmate would try to get home without getting caught. So, the warden, who had a pink Cadillac, jumped in his car and drove through the countryside, which was surrounded by corn fields. He figured that the inmate would use the cornfields as cover. Sure enough, a day after the escape, he spotted the inmate hitchhiking. So, he stopped to pick him up. The inmate jumped in, never thinking that a warden was driving a pink Cadillac. The inmate was shocked to see a gun pointed at his head. The warden drove him back to jail. Soon after that, the warden made the national news when Paul Harvey told the story of how the warden caught the inmate, within twenty-four hours, while driving his pink Cadillac.

I eventually worked in three different jails and each one generated some bizarre stories. One of the inmates was charged with bestiality, having sex with miniature ponies. Another female inmate had twins with her biological father. I was working in the ER one night when a corrections officer from a local jail called me and said that one of the inmates suddenly couldn't stand or move his legs. I didn't believe it, so I asked the officer to lift the inmate's leg and tell him to hold it up. He followed my instructions and said that the leg just fell down like dead weight. I said to transport him to the ER where I was working so that I could examine him. The guards brought the inmate to the ER, and without a doubt, the leg was numb and flaccid. I ordered a CT of his lower spine, expecting to find an unsuspecting lesion. Nothing showed up. So I went back and tested the inmate again. Now I was skeptical, and I felt he was faking it. So, I stuck a needle into the soles of both feet. He didn't even flinch, not a twitch of a muscle fiber. I was baffled and didn't know what to do; but, because the rest of the exam was unremarkable and because he didn't seem upset, I sent him back to jail and said I would check on him in the morning. The next day he was walking around as if nothing was wrong and never complained about it again.

The most bizarre case was the inmate caught with a jar of human toes found in his home. The inmate, I'll call RJ, was about fifty years old, a well-loved neighbor, a farmer, and a bachelor. It started out as a neighbor joking with him about having sex with his daughter. The inmate, RJ, said he would pay for the privilege and kill the daughter afterward so she wouldn't tell the police. The neighbor was shocked at his comment but made believe he would go along. Meanwhile he called the state police, and they said that they would set up a "hit man" for RJ so he wouldn't have to do the dirty work. On the designated day that RJ was to meet with the neighbor's daughter, he showed up with a jar of his sperm and a rope. He said that he wanted to hang the girl upside down and make her drink his sperm before he raped her. He was immediately arrested and put in jail. When I met him, I couldn't believe this meek middle-aged farmer, with a slight lisp, could have thought up such a sinister plot. When the state police went to his house, they found a jar of human toes. They were shocked and wondered who he had murdered. When questioned, he told them that he had cut off the toes from dead people in coffins at the funeral parlor. When he named who the deceased victims were, the authorities had to exhume the bodies to prove the toes were missing. He spent several years in jail on various charges.

In 1998 I started to moonlight at Andrew Kaul Memorial Hospital in St. Marys, Pennsylvania, and from the very first night I was impressed with the town. Unlike many other rural towns, St. Marys had a strong middle-class working population, one that I could relate to. The town was established in 1842 by German immigrants who wanted religious freedom. They called the town *Marenstadt*, in honor of the Virgin Mary. They were Bavarian Germans from the southern part of Germany, who were Roman Catholics. They encountered many hardships cutting down trees in a forest so dense that the fallen trees almost never hit the ground. Initially, lumber and coal were the main industries. Then other types of businesses developed, such as the manufacturing of clay pipes, and tanneries, and eventually the powdered metal industry became the major source of employment. The small town of St. Marys, hidden away in the Allegheny National Forest, developed into the carbon capital of the world and was also known as "a jewel in the woods." With unlimited employment opportunities, the town flourished due to its solid middle-class workforce.

The people were friendly, outgoing, and family oriented, like my Italian family and friends that I grew up with in New Jersey. I was confused at first, knowing that the town had a predominant German population, and Germans had the reputation as being stoic and reserved. My curiosity prompted me to research the ancestry of the Bavarian German immigrants, and I found out that the southern part of Germany was close to Italy, and the people remained Roman Catholic after the reformation. Also, I noticed that very few people in St. Marys fit the description of the stereotypical, tall, blond, Nordic race. Again, because Bavaria was close to Italy, there was probably intermarriage between Germans and Italians, which accounted for their shorter stature and darker hair.

One of the most amazing coincidences working in the St. Mary's ER was on a night shift. Up until that day the nearest hospital doing heart catheterizations was about thirty miles away. They only did elective diagnostic catheterizations, not emergent, because the cardiologists were not credentialed to stent blocked coronary arteries. If we had a cardiac emergency that needed stents or bypass surgery, the patient would have to be transported to Pittsburgh or Erie, both about two and a half hours away. Every few weeks I would ask the cardiologist when they would be certified to take emergency patients. One night before my shift in the ER, I called the cardiologist, Dr. A, at home, but his wife answered and said that he was out of town. She said that he would be back later that night and that she would tell him that I called. Later that night while working in the ER, I got a call from the cardiologist, Dr. A, who wanted to know why I called. I asked him if there was any progress made enabling his hospital to do emergency heart catheterizations. He said that he just got back from Chicago where he became certified to do emergency catheterizations. I asked him when we could send emergency cardiac patients to his hospital, in case they needed a stent. He said that, as of right then, we could send patients to him instead of transporting them on a two-and-a-half-hour trip to a tertiary center. Later that night, around three in the morning, I was sleeping in the doctors' lounge when the ER nurse called me with a patient, a sixty-year-old woman, who complained of back pain. I thought, *why would a patient have to come in the middle of the night for ordinary back pain?* I got up, and when I went to see the patient, the nurse was doing an EKG. I condescendingly asked, "Why are you doing an EKG for back pain? The nurse said because the patient complained that the pain radiated around to the front. I thought that was unnecessary and rolled my eyes until I saw that the EKG showed a definite inferior wall myocardial infarction. Thank God the nurse was diligent enough to consider the possibility that the woman was having a heart attack. What a coincidence that I had called Dr. A that night and established that he could do emergency cardiac catheterizations. Instead of transporting the woman to Erie or Pittsburgh, I was able to send her to Du Bois, only thirty minutes away. I called him immediately and transported the patient down to his hospital. I didn't know what happened to her until two days later when I was on my next shift and saw a note addressed to me. It was from Dr. A, and it said that the woman went into cardiogenic shock upon arrival, and he had to put in emergent cardiac stents to relieve the blockage. It saved her life—all because of a random phone call.

After moonlighting a few shifts in St. Marys, I became acquainted with some of the people and wished that I would have grown up in this town, married, and raised a family. At that time, I was 38-years-old, married, with a five-year-old daughter, Ali, and a two-year-old son, Chris.

It was about 20 years later, after a divorce, that I finally married a local woman and started a new family. That was about 12 years ago, and we have a daughter, Ella, 11 years-old, and a son, Max, nine years-old.

During the 33 years that I worked in St. Marys, I met many colorful characters. Several of the older men, all in their 80's, represented the image of the classic, hard-working American, with strong family and moral values. They exemplified the strong work ethic and backbone that St. Marys was noted for. These men were well respected, as well as legends in their community. They were my patients, and I got to know them over the years. Most lived up into their nineties. There was Knobby K., whose big smile drew your attention away from his one eye with a deformed pupil. He was well liked in the community and always pleasant when he came to the emergency department. Another was Merle L., who as a child had polio and sometimes went to school sitting on a wagon, pushing it with two wooden blocks. He had a great personality and didn't let his disability stop him, and as he got older, he was able to get around on crutches. He told me how he was shy with girls until one night at a high school dance. He said that he got his courage up and asked one of the prettiest girls to dance. He eventually married that girl, and they had three or four kids. He went on to be a member of the town council as well as a successful businessman. Because of the inability to use his legs, he only had his arms to get around, and therefore had developed phenomenal upper body strength. His hands were enormous, and his grip was like a vice. He said that he was able to do a pull up with one hand.

Another legend was an older man, named Friday, who was an acrobat in his younger days. I first met him when he was 80 years old, and he brought his wife to the emergency department for evaluation. He was only about five feet two inches tall, barrel chested, with wide shoulders, which was unusual for an 80-year-old man. I commented on his powerful appearance which prompted him to tell me about his acrobatic stunts performed in St. Marys and surrounding towns. I got to know him well, over the years, and was entertained by his stories. Whenever I mentioned his name, I found out that he was a legend, and almost everyone had heard of his acrobatic stunts. He said that at one time he was the only man in the world who could walk on his thumbs. He continued to lift weights at 86 years old, and he was still able to walk on his hands. I saw him occasionally and took him to the bar for a few beers. When he died unexpectedly, I was notified immediately, almost as if I were next of kin. Even the coroner asked me if I was satisfied that the cause of death was a cardiac event. A few days later, his stepdaughter called and invited me to his house, then offered me anything that belonged to Friday. I took a few pictures of him in his younger days doing acrobatic stunts, and I also took several ancient 25-pound barbell plates. I still use those plates, and think him often.

I went to Friday's wake and funeral and overheard someone mention where Friday was to be buried. Because he had no will or prior arrangements made, they naturally assumed he would be buried next to his wife. The dilemma arose when they found out that Friday had been married five times, and no one knew which of the five wives he would have chosen to be buried next to.

Friday's stepdaughter didn't know what to do with his beloved cat, Tom, and thought about calling the humane society to have him euthanized. No way! I knew how much Friday loved that cat, and as a friend I decided to do what was best for Tom. As a friend, I knew that's not the way Friday would want it, so I took his cat home with me. Tom was so sad that he didn't resist, and was easily transported to my house. When I opened the door of my vehicle, he jumped out and ran under it and wouldn't come out. I tried to entice him with cat food, but he was stubborn. Finally, he came out hours later after he burned the fur on his back from the exhaust pipe. We carried him into the house where he just moped around, refusing to eat or drink. After two days of his sad behavior we let him go out to see what would happen. After two days out, he came back to the house and became part of the family.

Going back to my third year of med school, at age 29, I came home in the summer and found rotations in New Jersey hospitals. I was so excited to arrange my first interview in Columbus hospital in Newark. I borrowed money from my mother and bought a suit and a pair of shoes so that I would look good at the interview. I had no car so I took two buses to get to the hospital, which was about an hour-and-a-half trip. I felt as though I was a celebrity making rounds in the hospital.

I had one bad experience, when I interviewed a patient with a severe hip problem. Initially the doctors that I had met gave me the freedom to interview their patients. Not knowing whose patient it was, I pulled a chart out of the rack and went to see the patient. Later that day an old doctor approached me and wanted to know who gave me permission to see his patient. I told him that all the other doctors said that I could randomly take charts out of the rack and see their patients. He started yelling that he never gave me permission and that I was forbidden to see any of his patients. Soon afterward I was called to the hospital's administrative office, where the CEO reamed me out for seeing a patient without the doctor's permission. I told him that I didn't know one doctor from the other and the ones that I spoke to all said that I was allowed to see any of their patients. He said that it was inexcusable seeing a patient without permission and that I could lose my rotation in his hospital and a note would be sent to my school. He warned me to watch my step, and if any other incident like that occurred I would be dismissed immediately.

Also during my rotation I had a 50 year-old patient, who I'll call Joe Pepper, who was admitted for a bleeding stomach ulcer. He had lost so much blood that he needed blood transfusions. When I interviewed him I asked if he was scared from seeing all the blood in his vomitus. He said no, it didn't bother him. I noticed while I was talking to him his voice sounded familiar from the distant past. It was possible because I had lived in the Newark area until I was six years-old. When I asked the nurses taking care of him if they knew his background, they said that years ago he had a run-in with the mob and was found in the hospital parking lot with several bullet holes in him. When I returned home that night I mentioned to my mother that I met a patient whose voice sounded familiar and his name was Joe Pepper. She immediately she recognized his name and said that his nickname is Nicky Irish and he was a good friend of my uncle Junior, the gangster. She said that when I was four and five years-old my uncle Junior took me around with him and he often visited Nicky Irish.

Going back to the beginning of my story, I mentioned my first-grade friend Robert, who started off our friendship by offering me a lady finger cookie. We kept in touch over the years, and I visited him and his family occasionally when I went back to New Jersey. We would call each other about four times a year. Then when we were both about sixty, I decided to call him for no particular reason.

When I called, his wife, Madeline, answered and said that Robert was sleeping because he had a terrible headache.

I said, "Madeline, that could be dangerous—wake him up! I need to talk to him!"

She went to wake him up and then came back to the phone and said that he couldn't talk because his head hurt too much.

I said, "Madeline, call 911 and get to the hospital ASAP, he is having a life-threatening bleed inside his head!"

The next day Madeline called me and said that he had emergency surgery to control the ruptured aneurysm and was doing well. Another coincidence in my life.

I have spent the last year-and-a-half writing my story, and now I've decided to wrap it up. I started writing it around age sixty-nine, because that's when I stopped working in the ER and had the free time to slowly peck away on my laptop. As I was typing and reflecting back over my lifetime, I entertained myself with the multiple unbelievable experiences for one man to have lived. Sometimes I would laugh at the ridiculous situations I got myself into, and other times I almost cried when I remembered the humiliation and disappointment that kept knocking me down. As I write this, I want to emphasize the philosophy that I mentioned in the beginning and have held onto all my life: "I can't be beat until I'm down and out and can't get up." That visceral, street-tough philosophy continued throughout my life, to weave the threads that formed the rope that pulled me up when I was down.

Was it luck, determination, or perseverance that allowed me to experience the kaleidoscope of events that squeezed into one lifetime? Sometimes I would like to think that I had a guardian angel watching out for me because I don't think that I had any extraordinary abilities, only the courage to go on, the determination to overcome my weaknesses, and the perseverance to continue. I'll never forget when I was seventeen and thought when I got older it would be a shame to have had a dream but never made the effort to pursue it. I said, "I'll never say, *IF it could have been,* or *IF only I would have* , and then look back with regrets."

I lived my life never knowing with any certainty that I was making the right decision, but I had the courage to pursue even the things that I feared. I can't say that I always believed in myself, because many times I doubted my ability to succeed. I was inspired by the stories of others who triumphed in spite of the odds stacked against them. There were those who overcame physical disabilities, others who were laughed at or discredited in their work, yet they had the wisdom and vision to pursue their dreams. To sum it up, it's not always the gifted nor the scholar that find fulfillment, but the ordinary individual with a dream, who perseveres while struggling along the way, and finally reaches their goal. In the end, *Perseverance is Omnipotent!*

About the Author

George Castellano was born in 1950 in Newark, New Jersey. He attended elementary and high school at St. Mary's in Rutherford, New Jersey, and graduated in 1968. He worked as a carpenter apprentice from 1969 to 1973, and served in the United States Air Force.

In 1976, George graduated from William Paterson College in Wayne, New Jersey, and attended medical school, Guadalajara, Mexico, from 1977 to 1981, and completed Fifth Pathway medical internship at Hackensack Medical Center in Hackensack, New Jersey in 1982. In 1982, now-Doctor Castellano moved to Johnstown, Pennsylvania, where he worked his surgical residency until 1986.

He started working in the ER full time in 1986, and became board-certified in emergency medicine in 1990, and worked in the ER until 2020.

In 2008, he moved to Kersey, Pennsylvania (and still lives there with his family today). He was jail doctor (1987 to present), 911 Medical director, Drug and Alcohol Medical director, Supervising Physician (monitoring physician assistants), Medical Director for the local schools, Ambulance Medical Director for four different ambulance services, and Occupational Health Supervising Physician.

George married Janel Struble in 2009, and they have two children, Ella, born in 2009, and Max, born in 2011. He has two grown children from a previous marriage, Ali and Chris.

Made in United States
North Haven, CT
02 July 2022

20886483R00095